James Johnson's first novel was like a meteor flashing across the black sky of evangelical fiction.

> Sherwood Wirt, Founder,
> Decision School of Writing,
> Minnesota

Jim sometimes was the only guy who looked out for and helped the guy who was down and out. He really cared. . . . He knew that I was hurting, and he did everything he could to keep me believing that I could do something.

> Will Norton, Jr., Dean,
> College of Journalism,
> University of Nebraska

Jim had been on the other side of suffering, so he knew what it felt like to hurt. He never lost his compassion for those in pain—whether physical, spiritual, or emotional.

> Marlene Minor, Deputy Associate
> Executive Director, World Relief,
> Resource Development Division,
> Wheaton, Illinois

He was one of the few whom I knew that had devoted his life wholeheartedly to the promotion of Christian literature, especially in the Third World. Jim liked and honored the principle of partnership in international cooperation among Christians.

> Timothy Yu, Publisher,
> The Rock House, Hong Kong

Jim played a key role in my life. . . . His excellency as a writer, and his honesty and transparency as a Christian, made a deep impression on me. . . . Jim was an encouragement as I began work with the Latin America Mission. Then he went to bat for me in trying to get published a manuscript about the Quichuas of Ecuador.

John Maust, Missionary and Editor of
The Evangelist, Latin America Mission

Jim was a model to me—a model of spirituality, a model of personal excellence, a model of great achievements. He always spurred people on to achieve the highest they could. . . . I benefited from and imbibed Jim's way of always striving to do better.

Richard Crabbe, Publisher,
Africa Christian Press, Ghana

I owe a deep debt of gratitude to Jim. . . . I took his correspondence course on Christian literature while still attending Bible college. While I was taking this course, the Lord clarified in my mind that I was to devote my life to His service in the field of communication. . . . Jim always expressed great interest in what I was doing and always encouraged me to excel in service for the Lord.

Paul Virts, Director,
Marketing Services,
Christian Broadcasting Network, Inc.

Jim was a true friend, both personally and also in the ministries of World Evangelical Fellowship. . . . The help that he gave me in getting one of my earlier books published was also deeply appreciated.

David Howard,
International Director,
World Evangelical Fellowship,
Singapore

He was a teacher, in formal and nonformal education, leading students on all continents from where they were to where they should be in understanding communication principles as they related to sharing the good news of the Lord Jesus.

H. Wilbert Norton, Sr.,
Former Executive Director,
Cameo Ministry of IFMA

Through Jim's life and testimony, many were challenged to become involved in missions. His efforts resulted in many nationals being trained to share the gospel through the means of literature.

Eric Bowley,
Director of International Ministries,
Back to the Bible

ISBN: 0-8024-7926-X

1 2 3 4 5 6 Printing/LC/Year 96 95 94 93 92

Printed in the United States of America

Servant of Words

A Tribute to James L. Johnson Mentor to Writers and Communicators

Robert B. Reekie, Editor

MOODY PRESS

CHICAGO

Contents

James L. Johnson (1927-1987)   9

Foreword   11
Kenneth N. Taylor

Preface   13
Robert B. Reekie

1. *Fun-Loving, Fast Paced*   21
Rosemary Johnson

2. *Missionary*   35
Earl O. Roe

3. *Teacher and Mentor*   47
Daniel V. Runyon

4. *The Novelist*   57
Jerry B. Jenkins

5. *Master Motivator*   65
Donald R. Brown

6. *Innovative Pastor*   75
Herbert and Phyllis Bailey

7. *Through an Editor's Eyes*   81
Judith E. Markham

8. *A Genuine Spirit*   97
     R. H. (Bob) Hawkins, Sr.

9. *Ruth, Keep Writing*   105
     Ruth Senter

10. *A Fellow Struggler*   121
     James F. Engel

11. *Visionary Strategist*   131
     H. Wilbert Norton, Sr.

12. *New Beginnings*   143
     Marlene Minor

13. *A Prophetic Voice*   157
     Ben Armstrong

14. *Following the Gleam*   165
     Jay E. Johnson

    Chronology   181

    Books by James L. Johnson   185

    "Jim's Last Word" and other articles   187
     James L. Johnson

James L. Johnson

1927-1987

*J*ames L. Johnson wrote fourteen books, including eight novels. He was born in Dollar Bay, Michigan, in 1927 and wrote his first short story when he was twelve. He was unusually gifted in leadership and communicated with clarity and precision. His sense of humor and love of people endeared him to thousands. His novel *The Death of Kings* (1973) is a widely acclaimed, towering example of excellent fiction writing. His Sebastian series of six novels continues to grip youthful and serious fiction readers. He served as a petty officer in the U.S. Navy for two years in the South Pacific. Then, in 1951, he became a Christian at twenty-five years of age. A year later he married Rosemary Lorts. After Bible school studies, he went to Nigeria as a missionary journalist and editor with the Sudan Interior Mission. That was followed by additional studies and a brief pastorate on the Near North Side of Chicago. He inspired Wheaton College to begin a graduate school of communication, where he played a key role as inspirer and a beloved professor. For almost twenty years he was fully absorbed in a worldwide Christian literature ministry as director of Evangelical Literature Overseas. Two years before his death he helped form a media training agency called Media Associates International, in Bloomingdale, Illinois. He was the recipient of many prestigious awards including the University of Michigan's McNaught Award for excellence in editorial writing and *Campus Life* magazine's award for excellence following publication of *The Death of*

Kings. He was an honorary member of the Mark Twain Society and in recognition of "outstanding editorial achievement" was made a life member of Kappa Tau Alpha journalism society.

James L. Johnson died in June 1987.

Foreword

*W*hat a pleasure it is for me to write a foreword to this book about my friend James L. Johnson.

Jim's life was one of single-hearted devotion to serving his Savior by writing about Him and by teaching others to write about Him, too. Many across the face of the earth are carrying on the ministry he taught them and remember their teacher with great respect, even awe.

I never had the privilege of sitting in on one of Jim's writing classes or seminars, and I am the poorer for it. Nor did I see as much of the brusque humor included in the fond memory of so many of his students and those who have written about him in this book. When Jim and I were together —he as executive director of Evangelical Literature Overseas and I as chairman of his board—I was with a man who thought straight to the point and then carried out our plans swiftly and expertly. That is not to say that I was not exposed to his wry repartee, for I had my full share of that, and that is part of what I so thoroughly enjoyed about him.

But perhaps above all was his sterling character along with his devotion to Christ and His kingdom, and to his students.

In these chapters you will read about a man who was a missionary, a teacher of graduate students, an editor, writer, and strategist.

I am grateful that I had the privilege of being Jim Johnson's friend.

KENNETH N. TAYLOR

Preface

*J*ames L. Johnson's credo as an author was *Ex Urbis et Imaginibus in Veritatem,* meaning From Shadows and Symbols into the Truth. But James L. Johnson was more than an author. His life and influence extended immeasurably beyond the pages of the fourteen books he authored and the hundreds of articles he wrote.

The men and women who write in this book provide a portrait of the man affectionately known as "Jim," as they saw and knew him. Their words are frank and sometimes unsparing about this man who made a difference in their professional and personal lives.

The composition of a book is a team effort and this book more so. Without the perceptive words by fourteen different writers, this book could not have happened. What these men and women share is not a composite biography; rather, it is a multifaceted portrait drawn with words by observers and beneficiaries of his life and work.

The contributors vary considerably in age. Some can look back over decades of professional life, and others have uncharted years of accomplishment ahead. The pages portray vivid memories of a man whose life made lasting imprints in their paths. Here the writers share Jim's qualities as husband, father, teacher, novelist, pastor, missionary, strategist, and friend.

The idea for the book goes back to late 1987. I am indebted to Greg Thornton, the general manager and publisher of Moody Press, for believing in the idea when it was first shared with him in June of 1989. Because of Jim Johnson's

lifetime affinity with Moody Memorial Church and appreciation for the Moody Bible Institute, we at Media Associates International are delighted that Moody Press agreed to work
with us to insure publication of a book about one of the ex-
ceptional people profoundly influenced by Moody ministries.

My sincere hope is that the word portrait of James L.
Johnson will not only reveal a true servant of God but become the threshold for young men and women seeking insight into God's working in a life given to the service of others
and the Lord Jesus Christ.

For those of us who knew him and cherished the friendship bond, Jim's death was numbing. A beloved, unique
friend and choice servant of God was snatched away in the
night, a voice silenced, and the flow of newly written words
terminated—forever halted.

Jim and I met early in the sixties at Winona Lake, In-
diana. From then on our professional association and personal friendship grew steadily. Throughout the twenty-five
years of companionship, Jim's personal awareness of God's
call was the hallmark of his life. One amazing dimension of
Jim's sense of mission was his ability to see opportunity in
the midst of uncertainty, to find alternatives when things were
bleak, to move on rather than tarry in the slough of despond.

We shared agonies, joys, and dreams—many times over
eggs and bacon at the Golden Bear Restaurant in Carol Stream
or the Olde North Pancake House on North Avenue, west of
Wheaton. A letter from Jim after one of those breakfast times
said, "Thanks for the breakfast and the good conversation.
We operate in a precarious world at best, but it's not half bad
when you don't have to go it alone. Thanks for being open to
my observations in various areas and also for standing by."

The agonies included what seemed to be the never-ending, tummy-grabbing concerns about finances; the disturbing
truth that the lack of financing often creates almost intoler-
able pressure upon servants of the Lord. In a letter written in
November 1975 Jim said, "Having funds allowed us to bring

the Wheaton College Communications Department key lecturers from the outside . . . the kind of people that build bridges to the student in terms of future careers. To get men and women such as Dick Ostling, religion editor of *Time* magazine, Phil Robison, religion editor of the *Chicago Tribune*, as well as Elizabeth Coining, Religious News Service, and Wes Pippert of UPI takes money. But their value cannot be measured in that sense totally because of our desire to keep students alive to career possibilities."

Even in the midst of money crunches, Jim thought of others and not himself. Once he wrote, "If you know anyone who is cashing in on 'E' bonds and has a little extra let me know. It seems I've managed to raise money for everybody else's travel to Hong Kong, but neglected to work on mine." In another letter carrying a May 1979 date Jim wrote, "I'm no longer taking a salary. We've got so much on our plate, and I'm waking up nights wondering why God won't give us the means to support the work."

Among the joys were the times of working together on ideas and plans for training Christian men and women who could make a difference in the quality and effectiveness of the print media. The sharing of dreams about working with national Christians on their local priorities or of helping shape an evangelism strategy that harnessed the media for the gospel remains as fresh in my memory as the morning dew.

Jim was driven ceaselessly by his commitment to Christian literature, which he called "the cause." Even while in the midst of his intense teaching schedule at the Wheaton College Graduate School, Jim cared about Evangelical Literature Overseas (ELO) and the inertia of the board to find a replacement. He wrote in October of 1974, "I'm taking the helm back again at ELO. I'm going to work it in with my other duties. Can't see sitting here waiting for somebody to take over—so I'm going to give ELO all I can, trusting not to bust any ventricles in the process. Light a candle for me now and then if you think of it."

Jim's walk with God was embedded in main street realities. His life was transparent and unmasked. He wrestled long and persistently with Christian truth and values in relation to life goals in everyday living.

Jim's concern for human tragedy and the untidy nature of society was inherent in his character. The black-white tensions and reality of American society impelled him to write, "No ingrained prejudice can be deleted except by collective thinking and responsibility. No other institution in society is more responsible for arbitrating societal differences and disputes of an interpersonal and intercultural nature than the church. The church can act decisively in cases of moral declension or the maligning of human values."

Because of his instinct for discovering talent, he would risk frequently for men and women he intuitively discerned as having potential. Jim constantly believed in others—always encouraging, challenging, goading, pushing, inquiring. His belief in the essential goodness and integrity of others was undying. As a result he would speak up in behalf of someone whose actions or words were less than noble or Christian. He understood humanness in a way few Christians do—maybe because he relied so heavily upon the mercy and grace of God to steer his life.

Jim was seldom strident in expressing his views, but that did not mean being silent on issues that plagued Christian agencies and mission endeavors. He abhorred macho Christian males who trod on others, whether men or women. He anguished over ethical flaws among Christian leaders and the politics that invades the inner sanctum of Christian motives, methods, and endeavors. And when he spoke candidly and compassionately his words were frequently ignored or rebutted. Jim unnerved some Christian leaders because of his incisive and penetrating insights about institutional agendas and programs operating in the Lord's name but seemingly devoid of holy motivation and cultural sensitivity.

If you had visited the Johnsons' basement room (he called it "The Hole"), where Jim spent countless hours putting words to his ideas and creating books, you would have found on the wall a sheet called "Markers of My Life." Among those markers are the words of Robert Louis Stevenson: "You can't run away from a weakness: you must sometime fight it out or perish: and if that be so, why not now, and where you stand?" And another, a poem by Carl Sandburg:

> Man is a long time coming
> Man will yet win
> Brother may yet line up with brother;
> This old anvil laughs at many broken hammers.
> There are men who can't be bought.

Words, excellent books, and writing were integral to the meaning of his life. Ever since writing his first short story as a boy of twelve, Jim loved and respected the story as a powerful instrument for truth—and after becoming a Christian, for the gospel.

Someone has said that the novel is the richest mode of communication ever devised. A novelist reveals much of himself that no other writer does. And Jim was no exception. His novels are models of what a Christian can get across by means of a well-told story. Yet Jim's conviction about the subtle power of the novel was never widely appreciated. "So many Christians back off from fiction as a form beneath them for communicating the gospel," he said in 1977.

Making a distinction between writing to publish and writing to change the course of history for somebody was part of Jim's writing philosophy. In a letter to Sherwood Wirt, who had asked Jim to speak at the Decision Writers' Conference, he said, "The extent of the distinction is considerable. And, unless we write with that difference in mind, we may get published, but we may not fulfill God's concern that our writing alter the course of someone's life. What kind of writing is that? I know what the difference meant to me; and I know where I got it. If it's okay, I'd like to challenge your writers with it."

Remarkably, that letter to Wirt is dated June 20, 1987, just five days before Jim died. He never got the chance to share that difference at the Decision Writers' Conference.

Jim's achievements through words are well known, and this book adds documentation to that fact. He appreciated and respected words and the potential power residing in a well-formed sentence, a choice phrase, a winsome word. He quoted as freely and frequently from great authors and poets as he did the great writers of the Bible. Every quote had unique personal significance for him. He never quoted to impress, but to express. One of his favorites was from an unknown source, and was the first listed under his "Markers of My Life":

> Is it so small a thing to have enjoyed the sun?
> To have lived light in the spring,
> To have loved, to have thought, to have done;
> To have advanced true friends and beat down battling
>   foes?

Jim's achievements were many. What was so remarkable was his pervasive humility. He never coveted accolades or sought recognition by the press, mission executives, academia, or his peers. In the words of the prophet Ezekiel, Jim stood in the gap wherever that was. His unfailing devotion to serve made him a modern-day Barnabas—one who could take on the strong and speak up for the weak or immature.

What Jim accomplished was done without ceremony. He truly was like the stage director who remains ever out of sight but whose role and presence is indispensable for those on the stage in the limelight.

Important to this book is the small selection of some of Jim's writing. The choices come from a rich array of his library of words. The problem was what to choose. The most poignant piece is "The Last Word," written by Jim in preparation for his memorial service that took place in the Barrows Auditorium of the Billy Graham Center in Wheaton on Sunday, June 28, 1987. Jim was also a powerful and inspirational teacher of writers and would-be writers. Furthermore, he articulated with the precision of a practitioner the technical side of his writing craft. To illustrate his gift, we have included two of the many articles he put together to help fledgling writers learn their craft and aid mature ones in improving their craftsmanship.

I want to thank Kenneth Taylor for his foreword. Dr. Taylor's friendship and vision were cherished by Jim. To Rosemary Johnson and their son, Jay, I express gratitude for their encouragement and invaluable suggestions for this book. And to Leota Meyer, who worked alongside me in the preparation of the chapters for publication, and to Sharyl Sieh, who processed the thousands of words represented by the chapters, my sincere thanks.

Like the mysteries he loved to create, he himself embodied a mystique I dearly loved and needed to decipher from time to time.

1
Fun-loving, Fast-paced

Rosemary Johnson

Rosemary Johnson lives in Wheaton, Illinois. She works at Gorman's LA-Z-BOY in computer accounting. She enjoys swimming, fitness programs, gardening, crafts, reading, travel, and her pet golden retriever, Sydney Sebastian.

*I*t was a perfect evening in early June 1952 as our families and friends gathered for the wedding rehearsal.

Perfect? But, where was the groom? (He was here just a moment ago.)

"He will be back shortly," said Paul, one of the groomsmen. "He just had a little nosebleed."

"What happened—is something wrong?" I anxiously inquired as Jim came into the chapel.

"No, no, I'm fine. I don't know, it just came out of the blue." He shrugged.

"A likely story, Johnson."

"Tell us another," they teased.

"So, well, you see, there was this guy," the happy storyteller began as he had done so many times previously, capturing my heart with his great sense of humor and unlimited, wordy yarns.

Little did I realize, it was just the beginning of a story-filled, fun-packed, fast-paced, uphill-downhill, adventurous partnership, albeit lonely at times, but rewarding thirty-five years with this good-looking, blue-eyed hunk of nervous energy with whom I was willing and eager to pledge my love.

We happily settled into our Astor Street/Gold Coast small basement apartment (that was all we could afford in that area) on the Near North Side of Chicago. It was cozy and conveniently located near our places of employment and our church life. Moody Bible Institute (MBI) was also close by, where Jim decided to take some Bible study courses in their evening school program.

It was during the annual Missionary Conference at Moody Memorial Church in 1955 that we learned of a need in Nigeria, West Africa.

"Say, Jim, I understand you enjoy writing and editing. How about helping us out in Africa?" said a missionary friend.

"Who, me?" a startled Jim replied. "Oh, well, I don't know. I'd have to think about it—I haven't finished my studies at MBI yet."

"Well, we need to relieve the editor of our mission publication in Nigeria, so please give it some serious consideration."

In a few short months, after much prayerful discussion, we found ourselves at the Sudan Interior Mission (SIM) headquarters in New York where we were to spend some time getting acquainted. There were medical and various other tests required for overseas service. Each morning we gathered for prayer and study and some work-activity instructions for the day.

"Jim, there's a leaky faucet in the bathroom on the second floor. You will find tools at the end of the hall. Please see what needs to be done," said the man in charge.

A perplexed Jim turned to me, "Honey, did I hear that right?"

"Well, I don't know exactly. Let's go see what needs to be done in the bathroom."

With each new task of needed maintenance, Jim would become frustrated, fussing, and fuming, "Why doesn't SIM ask me to speak, write, and edit? That's what I know. Why this stuff?" I began to realize the compelling, driving force and urgency within him to get on with the work he felt called to do.

Of course, anything that needed fixing, forget it, call the repair man! Jim was into creative writing, speaking—that's where the action was! I soon became "the fix-it wife" when things needed attention. An "action and fix-it team": a good combination was taking shape.

During our physical exams the doctor at the New York mission headquarters was puzzled.

"Jim, your blood pressure keeps going too high at times. Has this happened before and very often?"

"Oh, yeah, well, yes and no—you see, it just acts up like this, then its OK again."

The doctor, obviously concerned, suggested some medication to help the problem.

"Do you think we will really pass muster and meet all medical tests and other requirements?" we kept asking each other.

"Maybe, just maybe, we won't really qualify."

"Yeah, might be just as well."

Doubting, questioning God! Unnerved, praying, hoping for what, we didn't know.

For the time being we came to realize that the weeks in New York were a necessary training procedure to prepare us to be all things and do all things, even if it was a difficult straining-at-the-bit experience for Jim.

With acceptance into the SIM family came confidence, and we were on our way to the mission field. We had only to believe and trust that our loving God who had brought us this far would be ever near and guide us in meeting our needs whatever they might be.

We stepped off the plane in January 1956 at Lagos, Nigeria, West Africa. A puzzled, excited Jim exclaimed, "Honey, look at all those people—what a welcome!"

Much to our chagrin, we were informed by the "few" co-workers, who were there to greet us, "They are expecting Queen Elizabeth of England for a royal tour of the colony."

What an introduction to this, our adopted land!

We loved our time getting to know the people, their culture, and their land as we were sent up country, inland from coastal Lagos to study the language. They were a patient, gracious people as we struggled with their tonal words.

"My 'Iyawo' and I went to market yesterday." The Africans started to smile, as Jim continued to preach one Sunday morning. They loved his silly stories and examples, especially when he used the wrong tone as we were learning the new language. They just couldn't contain themselves any longer as they burst out with laughter. Wife and monkey are the same word, *Iyawo,* with a different tone. What a time we had with such wonderful people.

"Jim, don't move, lie perfectly still," I warned as I spotted a deadly snake coiled up in the mosquito netting of our bed just above his head. I ran for help, and a brave young African lad came and disposed of the creature promptly.

"Oh, look, Jim, a real live scorpion! See, right there by your shoe!" (Our new co-workers on the mission compound had their "scorpion-trophies" pickled in a jar.) I just had to have one, too!

"It's going that way if you want to think you can catch it," said he, as I slapped a jar over it, holding it in place. The next morning we discovered it was "with family." No wonder it was so easy. How could we possibly pickle this mother and babies when we wanted a family so badly of our own?

I was getting acquainted with the tropics and learning that this brave missionary hubby, with all of his bold air of authority, could not abide anything crawly or creepy—especially when it wasn't where it was supposed to be.

As each new day and experience unfolded we were profoundly aware of God's blending Jim and me for our preservation and His purposes in our lives.

We were in Nigeria for three years. When Jim recalled those days in *Coming Back*, he wrote:

The Africans understood us well. They knew I had too much steam and they took the time to be safety valves. We found them a gentle people. While I fumbled trying to edit a big African monthly magazine, they treated us as if we did everything right. We shall never forget these kind and helpful people.

In three years we were home, wiser, beaten up from the tropics and trying to learn too much in a short time. We were exhausted and disappointed at feeling little accomplishment. I felt I had failed the Africans and even God. Missionaries go for a lifetime. We had put in three years, and were never to go back again. What had we achieved in those short years, beyond the experience of knowing the great heart of Christianity in the African people?

In late 1958, in fragile health from pressures of the work and excessive heat, we returned to the States and settled into the pastorate of Elm-LaSalle Street Church on Chicago's Near North Side.

It was a happy Jim in the pastoral ministry. After completing his studies at MBI, he was ordained in 1960. We were blessed with a warm and loving church family. But still there was one thing missing.

A child of our own.

We couldn't understand why we were being deprived of this special fulfillment and enjoyment. After learning of no apparent medical reason, we resigned ourselves that it was just not to be. Then in December of 1960 we received a card from a missionary family friend with news of the birth of their second child. I found myself on my knees, weeping out my frustration in prayer, pleading, "Why, God, it's just not fair! She has two and we have none, why? Please God, why not one for us, too?"

Within a very short time, we were delirious with happiness when the doctor confirmed the good news: we would indeed have a child. A miracle in answer to a desperate prayer, no less! Happy, with family on the way and Jim anticipating new studies, we moved in 1961 to Ann Arbor and the University of Michigan where Jim could work on his journalism degree. (He had completed a two-year program at Suomi College in Hancock, Michigan, after coming home from his service in the navy in late 1940s.) He was now anxious to complete this phase of study to be better prepared for his life work.

One beautiful fall day in 1961, feeling the first signs of birthing pains, I dashed to the phone to locate Jim at the university. He dropped everything (probably literally!) and rushed home to drive me to the hospital.

Later in the evening as I struggled with delivery (it was a late-in-life production) and with anxious doctors in attendance, I wondered, *Where was Jim?* I hoped he was OK.

Of course I was sure he was just outside the door, pacing the floor, wringing his hands, and muttering to anyone who would listen to his anxious concerns. Wrong! I later learned he was off in some far corner with his books and assignments. He had to get away. He couldn't bear the anxiety of it all. Oh, dear hubby and father-to-be!

When he saw our blue-eyed baby boy, Jim was beside himself with pride, exclaiming, "He'll never get those feet off the ground!" He was a happy papa, enjoying sharing the care and feeding of our new son, Jay. In later years he was a proud father in seeing Jay grown to be a tall good-looking young man in his own right and indeed getting those feet off the ground as well as having them firmly planted toward his own goals in life.

In 1963 Jim prepared for graduation. He was happy with his completed studies. He had been honored by the University of Michigan with the McNaught Award for Excellence in Editorial Writing. But we were uncertain about our next move. It was at that time we were pleasantly surprised by a visit from Kenneth Taylor, Peter Gunther, and Harold Street, directors of Evangelical Literature Overseas (ELO), an organization located in Wheaton, Illinois.

The men presented the needs of ELO's growing program of literature distribution and overseas work and invited Jim to join them in their endeavor. We believed this to be a timely leading in answer to our prayerful concern. So our happy family of three was on the move again, this time to Wheaton, a western suburb of Chicago.

Jim learned and experienced much in the ensuing years with ELO, traveling, speaking, and fund-raising for the many needy projects overseas. He also pursued his love for fiction writing in his spare time with the hopes of some published work of his own. He was overjoyed when his first novel, *Code Name Sebastian,* was published in 1967 and was well received by readers of various ages.

In 1968 Jim's initiative and vision helped found the Communications Program of the Wheaton College Graduate School. At last he was fulfilled in his love with words and the written page, teaching the students and seeing the new program through the growing pains.

"The hour is late, don't you think you ought to call it quits for tonight?" I would plead as he would start to critique yet another assignment from one of his students.

"Yes, yes, I'm coming. They are good, but they can do better. I want to help them to see it differently."

How could I scold or try to coax Jim to do otherwise? He loved doing it all, and in the doing he exercised and sharpened his own skills.

His many trips abroad enabled him to see and feel firsthand what was important for accurate, descriptive writing and to completely pour himself into his characters. He especially loved the ongoing development of the Sebastian series. He so wanted to continue them beyond the sixth book of the series.

Jim probably wrestled the most with his novel *The Death of Kings* because of its different sensitive issues. He wanted to present a true picture without offense to anyone.

Belonging to the Book-of-the-Month Club and Literary Guild of America, he liked to keep abreast of all the latest best-sellers. He was a fast reader, and his bedside night-stand, without fail, contained three or four volumes in the process of being consumed. How he could absorb so much, I'll never know!

Among his favorites would be works by Leon Uris, James Michener, and Alistair MacLean. His old-time favorites were Robert Louis Stevenson, Carl Sandburg, and Alfred Tennyson. He had before him on his study wall his credo as an author: *Ex Umbris et Imanginibus in Veritatem*—From Shadows and Symbols into the Truth.

Someone once asked me what was Jim's favorite Scripture verse or text. I'm really not sure he had one in particular. He liked to draw from every portion equally. But if there ever was a verse, it could well be the one he had framed and hanging in his office, taken from Philippians 4:6-7 (RSV)*: "Have no anxiety about anything, but in everything by prayer and supplication with thanksgiving, let your requests be known to God and the peace of God which passes all understanding shall keep your hearts and minds in Christ Jesus."

Even though Jim was the youngest of his family of six siblings, in later years, with both parents gone, he became like a big brother to the rest of them, always calling with his concern and encouragement and making himself available when and where he could in their various times of need.

Likewise, when there came a time of need in my family, this big, soft-hearted, generous man welcomed my mother into our home without hesitation. She had become semi-invalid from a stroke, and for the last six years of her sojourn here she lived with us. She and Jim shared a love for words and the written page, enjoying a good sense of humor in each other. He never complained when the care of her increased as she became bedridden. It took extra time and energy from

* *Revised Standard Version.*

the family, but he always understood with caring encourage-ment. He was supportive and found the necessary time to help with all the final arrangements when she died. I shall be forever grateful for the heart of gold in this partner God had given me.

In the late 1970s, with Jim busily engaged in teaching, administrating, and writing, we were confronted with new needs within our family. Bone weary and heart-stressed from all the extra involvement, there was not much energy left for interaction on the home front. As Jim became more absorbed in creative and work pressures, I floundered in my introverted self to make up the difference, making Jay's developing teen years difficult.

I needed Jim's old vocal, joking self, and he needed more input from me. What had happened to the lively, joking, easy bantering that came to us so naturally in former years? How often we permit the pressures of life to stifle the joy of loving relationships.

We seemed helplessly caught in the net of misreading each other's needs. Ginger, our adorable beagle, with her all-knowing expressive, soulful eyes—"People, ugh!"—was a good outlet with her own special concerns.

With an air of self-confidence, bravado, and aggressive manner Jim provided good cover for his insecurities and vul-nerabilities—probably misunderstood by many, as few got beyond that cover. Only to those closest to him would he permit that insight. Like the mysteries he loved to create, he himself embodied a mystique I dearly loved and needed to decipher from time to time. What I needed to realize was that communication between us did not depend on words but on being together.

What holds lives together during stressful times? By God's merciful love and grace our love for each other proved to be a commitment strong enough to pull us through the down times. Like scores of other overextended husbands and fathers, Jim was guilt-ridden about the brevity of time given to his family and home life. Yet within the written page he left a legacy of loving devotion and provision.

"Jim, I think I'll go over to that new sport center and see what the pool is like. Want to come?"

"Yeah, can't right now though, maybe tomorrow, yes, for sure tomorrow."

He did join me from time to time and found swimming beneficial. But then he didn't keep it up with the frequency that would help relieve those hyperactive, stress-filled days. There was just "no time" anymore for that sort of thing. He misplaced (or hid?) my house keys one morning with the subtle suggestion, "Let's not get carried away with all of this swimming and workout stuff."

"Come, Jim, come with me."

"Can't this morning, hon, got a meeting to get to. Maybe tonight."

No amount of coaxing or scolding would do the trick. One time he did go with me to a swim meet I had entered for the fun of competing. He brought a book along. The delays were boring, so I couldn't blame him.

"Time's-a-wasting"—and at a swim event, no less!

"You did great, but you were too slow on takeoff—you need to do thus and thus!" Oh, help, I was looking for only the glad-hand stuff. Little did I realize it was his caring, challenging remarks that drove me to try harder, making him proud of a few wins in later meets.

We had a rustic cabin deep in the woods of Michigan we all loved to retreat to. Jim would find himself revived and renewed. They say creative people need a place of isolation to hibernate and do battle with words and character plots in their writing endeavors.

"Jim, dinner's ready."

"OK, be there in a sec."

"So, what do you think, would you like to do that or—"

"Hmm, oh that, yeah I guess."

Present in body, but far away in some deep story or perhaps palaver of the day's business.

His cabin in the woods by the lake and Ginger at his feet was the good life for this man of perpetual motion. Alas, that too often became shelved as the all-too-short forty-eight-hour weekends didn't allow enough time from the study-hole to travel up to Michigan.

In early 1978 warning signs of a truly stressed-out heart began to increase and became a serious concern during his visits to the doctor.

"Jim, you can do one of two things. You can have this heart bypass and return pretty much to your usual schedule, or you can cut your activities in half and get used to the rocking chair the rest of your life."

"What a choice, doctor, thanks a lot."

He finally had to acknowledge that he really had no choice and knew he had to take time for this much needed surgical repair.

In 1978 God saw fit to bring him through that horrendous, frightening ordeal. When all hope for his recovery was gone, with the prayers of the dedicated medical staff and scores of friends, he was back. After some months of recuperation he was again ready to tackle life and find his place in the communications arena.

When he had to forgo his love for teaching in 1982, he joined World Relief Corporation. Through his writing, speaking, and traveling he shared the realities of the needy world.

In May 1985, he, Jim Engel, and Bob Reekie founded Media Associates International (MAI), an agency set up to focus entirely on training national Christian writers and indigenous publishers throughout the world. Time ran out for Jim and his contribution to that cause, but I can hear him say, "It's in good hands, carry on, carry on!"

He was thankful for the nine plus years following heart surgery, speaking, writing, and publishing in the work he loved. God spared him to see Jay graduate from high school and college; but sadly, Jim was prophetic in thinking he was asking God too much to see Jay graduate from seminary. How proud Jim would have been to see his son finish seminary and be ordained and absorbed with his very own parish ministry.

The one-hundred-year celebration of his hometown, Dollar Bay, Michigan, to be held on July 4, 1987, was a special event he happily anticipated. He considered it an all-time honor to be asked to deliver the main address and write the town history book. He looked forward to seeing all the family and hometown folk to be gathered there. That was not to be.

Just nine days prior, on June 25, 1987, Jim passed from this life, as he lived it, fast. In a blinking of an eye, he was gone.

From the beginning, Jim accepted the Nigerians on our staff as friends, peers, and colleagues. Without condescension or fanfare, Jim took time on the job to provide hands-on training to his fellow staffers whenever possible.

2
Missionary

Earl O. Roe

Earl O. Roe is a former missionary to Nigeria, where he was
assistant editor of *African Challenge* magazine. He is now senior
editor of Regal Books in Ventura, California, with forty years of
experience in writing and editing. In the early sixties he worked to
establish West Africa's first accredited four-year school of
journalism at the University of Nigeria, then called Jackson
College of Journalism, now the department of mass
communication. He lives in Santa Paula, California.

*J*im Johnson. The name always brings a smile to
my face—and to my heart. For such are my memories of this
marvelous, multifaceted man.

I first met Jim Johnson in January 1956 when he and
Rosemary flew into Ikeja International Airport, some ten miles
outside Lagos, Nigeria's capital city. Rousing pomp and ceremony enveloped the pair as they stepped from their plane
onto the tarmac that day and were greeted with all the splen-
didly regal panoply the city could muster. Traditional rulers,
political leaders, and other assorted dignitaries were all around
them, while contingents of the nation's armed forces and national police paraded and drilled nearby. And just beyond the
host of marching men, a fleet of military jets was drawn up in
formation beside the runway.

The Johnsons barely had time to enjoy their spectacular
reception before learning that they had arrived at the capital's
airport on the eve of a three-week royal tour of the colony by
Queen Elizabeth II and Prince Philip of England.

Rosemary was quietly delighted, and Jim was enormously
amused by the regal grandeur. As they cleared customs, they

spotted our delegation from Niger-Challenge Press waiting quietly in the background to receive them. Jim grinned, laughed, and exclaimed, "Wow, is this how you welcome all the new missionaries here?" Taking our cue from his tongue-in-cheek question, we replied that yes, elaborate receptions for missionaries were commonplace here.

Jim, a Christian journalist and professional writer, came to be editor of *African Challenge,* the mission's nondenominational magazine. The *Challenge* already enjoyed a wide West African circulation in two editions, one in English and the other in the local vernacular language, Yoruba.

When Jim came on board, I had been working at the *Challenge* for two years, serving as assistant editor, news editor, and "Uncle Joseph," the children's editor. I liked Jim immediately. An extroverted and congenial man, he was refreshingly free of pretense, and his naturalness was a joy to all of us. Considerate and fair, he proved to be a great boss, mentor, and powerful motivator of those who served with him.

Jim's drive was awesome; he frequently set a pace that was breathtaking, for he possessed a nervous, restless energy that never let him slow down. Seemingly almost driven at times, Jim brimmed ceaselessly with ideas for new stories and features and always had a dozen projects in development at any given time.

Yet he never struck me as tense or pressured. He just seemed to be a highly motivated, genuinely enthusiastic man. Full of life and the sheer joy of being alive, he simply operated in one gear—high—as though there were not going to be enough years for him to accomplish all that he hoped and wanted to do in a single lifetime.

In those days Jim was long, lanky, and angular. He had the build and look of a long-distance runner. And when he walked, the legs of his trousers sometimes moved as though they were unoccupied. Very physical and animated when he talked, Jim gestured energetically with his hands while speaking, drawing pictures in the air.

He enjoyed a good joke and laughed easily, guffawing heartily over anything that really tickled him. Though more restrained than Jim, Rosemary fully shared his sense of humor and zest of life. They were assigned a small apartment next to mine in a two-story building, so I occasionally dropped by in the evening to visit with them.

More than once I arrived to find the two of them standing astride their living room couch, holding hands and bouncing up and down while they laughed over a private joke or rejoiced over some good news they had just received. And just as often, I would find them in quieter moments, sitting together in their living room, talking or reading, as they listened to a favorite record, frequently the Norman Luboff Choir singing cowboy favorites.

My apartment had a small second-floor balcony, and beneath it I had planted a blood-red bougainvillea. Its branches twined through the second floor balcony railing. My balcony was only a few feet from the Johnson's bedroom window. I was not aware that a large branch of the magnificent bougainvillea had grown over and around their window. One day during an afternoon siesta, a huge snake, several feet long, spiraled up the vine, detoured out on the stray branch and slithered in through the Johnson's open window. Since the day was a bit cool and the snake felt in need of a little warmth, it slid up a bed leg and stretched out full length between the sleeping Johnsons, who were lying back to back on top of the bed.

Suddenly, Rosemary's screams, Jim's shouts, and the sounds of heavy blows awakened me. I sat up startled. What was happening? It certainly sounded like Jim was beating Rosemary, but that made no sense. They were crazy about one another. Besides, they were missionaries!

Rushing out on the balcony I saw Jim bolt from his front door and head for my place, machete in hand. Dear heaven, had this good man gone strangely berserk? Astonished, I watched as he attacked my beautiful bougainvillea and, in moments, slashed it to the ground.

Then Jim told me what happened. He and Rosemary had awakened from their siesta and—fortunately—each got out on separate sides of the bed. As Rosemary turned around to smooth out the covers, she saw the snake, still lying contentedly in the warm bed. Her screams of horror caused Jim to whirl around in puzzled alarm, until he also saw the snake. Shouting in surprise, he flipped the bedclothes over the creature and clubbed it to death through the bedding.

During our time together in Nigeria, I covered only a few story assignments on the road with Jim before I discovered we shared a common failing: neither of us had any sense of direction. All our lives we had steered by road signs, landmarks, and the like. But in the bush, Nigeria's unpaved laterite (red decayed rock) roads seldom went straight for any distance and none bore road signs. Every thatched hut, cassava patch, and palm tree we came to looked like every other we had passed.

So we paused at every fork and road junction we came to. Had we passed here before? Possibly yes, probably no. Should we turn left or right or go straight ahead? Sometimes we followed his hunches and sometimes mine. But always we were wrong.

We learned early to allow extra time for travel if tackling an assignment meant leaving the environs of Lagos. We carried a thermos of coffee and a bag lunch or some shillings with which to bargain for food when we ended up somewhere totally lost, silly with weariness, and terribly hungry.

We finally conceded that we were hopelessly incapable of developing road smarts and took to traveling with either a Yoruba companion, a staff colleague, one of the pastors, or a cook-steward who knew the area, the people, and the country.

Under Jim's leadership and direction, the *Challenge* achieved a pan-African circulation in every English-speaking country, with limitations in South Africa. Because of their apartheid policies, some issues of the *Challenge* were banned or confiscated. For much of the 1950s, the *African Challenge* was Africa's largest-circulation, English-language magazine, outselling its closest competitor, the popular secular magazine, *Drum*.

Ever mindful that we missionaries on the staff were writing for a readership whose culture differed from our own, Jim was concerned that the *Challenge* should be written well and genuinely communicate to its readers. And since the magazine was widely used as a reading aid in schools, it had to provide solid information that was educationally sound and geared to the school-age reader. At the same time, the magazine had to have a certain amount of content geared to adults who bought and read it.

Because we were a publication with an evangelical emphasis, he ensured that the gospel of Jesus Christ was always clearly and simply presented for the unsaved. And he saw that every issue contained additional material to encourage, inspire, and nurture the reader who was already a believer, because *Challenge* magazine was often the only Christian literature that many believers could afford. By inviting and utilizing African input in these efforts, Jim developed a keen sense of what would or would not work for our readership.

So working with Jim in this intercultural publishing endeavor was an education in itself for me, an opportunity that enabled me to gain invaluable hands-on experience and knowledge. Being a competent professional, Jim pursued his craft and his responsibilities with seriousness, though he never took himself seriously. He shunned pedestals and worked unaffectedly with all of us on the staff, nationals and expatriates alike. To each of us he was a true friend and a genuine brother in Christ.

From the beginning, Jim accepted the Nigerians on our staff as friends, peers, and colleagues. Though Jim labored intensely, because he was gregarious and good-humored he established a relaxed, easygoing relationship with the Nigerians, particularly with those who worked shoulder-to-shoulder with us in the editorial and production departments of the magazine.

Generally cheerful, fun-loving, enthusiastic, and eager to learn, our Nigerian staff responded to Jim with affection and appreciation. They knew that Jim respected and enjoyed them, that he believed in them and in their potential. And without condescension or fanfare, Jim took time on the job to provide hands-on training to his fellow staffers whenever possible. He knew that, given the opportunity and training, our *African Challenge* colleagues could do anything and everything we were doing—and probably do it better, since they would be communicating with their own people.

In theory, a good missionary works himself out of a job as quickly as possible by imparting his knowledge and expertise to Christian nationals so they can take over from him when they are ready. In this way the original work becomes indigenous, enabling the nationals to exercise ownership over the ministry as they assume responsibility for it. Then the missionary can work in some other ministry.

During my first years in the literature ministry in Nigeria I was dismayed to find no real commitment to the training of Nigerians. In fact, within our mission and in our compound, I encountered resistance and hostility toward any talk of indigenizing our endeavors. If anything, we missionaries appeared to be entrenching ourselves for an indefinite stay, manifesting no real intent to hand the ministry over to Christian nationals in the foreseeable future. A blind faith in Western ways, an oft-voiced belief in white superiority, and a visible contempt for African intellect and character by some missionaries undergirded these hardened attitudes.

Yet I was not long in Nigeria before realizing that the knowledgeable African shared none of the Western world's veneration for Dr. Albert Schweitzer and his well-known medical work at Lambarene, Gabon. I was really puzzled, until a

Nigerian civil servant said, "Schweitzer was a medical doctor. But how many doctors did he train during the time he was in Gabon? Not one! He never passed on to a single African the knowledge and skills that were his. He was paternal and patronizing."

So as Jim's assistant editor on the *African Challenge,* I was delighted to discover that we shared a common concern: the need to pass on to Christian nationals whatever training, skills, and knowledge we possessed, so that they would be qualified to carry on the ministry. In this respect, Jim is on record as saying, "Our task is to work with national Christian writers . . . they alone can reach their own people with the right words."

Jim agreed that it was actually much easier to make a writer out of a Nigerian with the necessary aptitude than to make "Nigerians" out of us missionaries. Though we were trained and skilled, we were ignorant of African culture generally, were uneducated in the idioms of its people, and were uninformed on those issues of primary importance to those for whom we hoped to publish—and no amount of goodwill on our part could offset those inherent disadvantages.

Jim's efforts to establish an in-house training program were resisted by those heading our publishing endeavor. However, Jim quietly carried on with his commitment, his subtle efforts becoming something of an underground operation. In this regard, he was of immense encouragement to one of our national pastors, Luckson Ejofodomi, who worked in the editorial departments of both the Yoruba and the English editions of the *Challenge.*

Though Luckson had a secondary school education and had earned a Bachelor of Theology degree from Igbaja Seminary in Ilorin, Nigeria, he had no formal training in journalism. But he was a born communicator with a genuine gift for words. A veritable linguist, he could speak and write in several languages, including Urobo, Itsikiri, Ibo, Yoruba, and English and some Edo. Jim believed that Luckson should have greater exposure for his writing skills in addition to the occasional assignment he was given at the *Challenge*. An opportunity soon opened.

At that time in the mid-1950s, the *Lagos Sunday Times* carried a pastor's devotional column, written by a different clergyman or missionary each week. And since our Niger Challenge Press compound was full of clergy and missionaries, the *Times* periodically approached our staff, usually through the compound manager, asking us to write for this column. Since many of our missionaries were not comfortable as writers, and since Jim and I, as editors, were assumed to be writers also, we were frequently asked to provide the column.

Up to this time, none of our Nigerian staff, pastors included, had ever been permitted to write this column when the *Challenge* was asked to provide it. So Jim suggested to me that, whenever it was his turn or mine to write the column, we quietly pass the opportunity on to Luckson and invite him to write the feature for the *Times*. I agreed wholeheartedly.

The column was never bylined, no matter who wrote the weekly devotional, so it appeared anonymously week after week. Consequently, no one knew for a while, apart from the three of us, that Luckson—not Jim nor I—was doing the writing. Then one day, the *Sunday Times* editor called our compound manager and asked, "Hey, what are you folks doing there at the *African Challenge* that is making such a difference here?"

Our manager asked what he meant.

The *Times* editor explained that the pastor's column normally had a rather ho-hum mail response when it appeared. But lately, whenever it was written by a *Challenge* staffer, the mail pull was enormous—and all of it favorable. Our manager was unable to explain why readers were now responding more than before, so he asked Jim about it.

And Jim, beaming broadly, said, "The difference is Luckson Ejofodomi. He's been writing the pastor's column lately.

Earl and I haven't written one for a long time. Luckson's writing is making the difference, because the readers recognize that the writer is someone who knows and understands them.

"Because Luckson is one of them, he's on target when he addresses their needs and concerns. Earl and I try, but we're not Nigerians. We don't strike the familiar chords that Luckson does. When he writes for them, they recognize that they are reading the words of a kindred spirit."

Jim's words caused much displeasure among the missionary staff but great jubilation among the Nigerian staff. After that, while we remained on the staff, Luckson or one of the other Nigerian pastors on the *Challenge* staff wrote the pastor's column for the *Sunday Times*. The impact of Luckson's writing upon the readers of the nation's then largest weekly newspaper had vindicated Jim and proved his thesis: "National Christian writers . . . alone can reach their own people with the right words."

Jim's leadership and influence upon both Luckson and me had further implications. Desiring that Luckson have an opportunity for formal training, Jim, after returning to the States in 1958, personally approached Robert Laubach, then president of Laubach Literacy, Inc. (LLI) and a professor in the Syracuse University School of Journalism—now the Newhouse School of Mass Communications—and recommended Luckson as a candidate for a Laubach Literacy scholarship. As a result, Luckson received the *only* undergraduate scholarship award ever given by LLI.

Some of Luckson's former missionary colleagues were outraged. One expressed the opinion, "What a waste. Luckson can never be anything more than an office boy." But Luckson did so well at Syracuse University that he was admitted to Sigma Delta Chi, the journalism honorary society, in his first year. And after obtaining his B.A. from Syracuse in 1962, he went on to earn both an M.A. (1964) and a Ph.D. (1974) from Boston University.

While earning his doctorate, Luckson served at various times on the faculties of Boston University, Tufts University, and Harvard University. Upon receiving his Ph.D., he became an assistant professor in the Black Studies Department of the University of Massachusetts from 1974 to 1977 and chairman of the department from 1975 to 1977. In 1978, Luckson returned to Nigeria and joined the faculty of the Department of History at the University of Ibadan, the premier university of Nigeria.

After the Johnsons left Nigeria in 1958, Jim never lost sight of his goal to provide opportunities for training Christian nationals. His two decades of leadership at Evangelical Literature Overseas (now part of Media Associates International, Inc.) and years of pioneering the communications department of Wheaton College Graduate School are testimony of his dedication to provide training and educational opportunities to others.

Inspired by Jim's belief in indigenous leadership training and by his personal example, I also went to Syracuse University and studied for a master's degree in journalism to academically qualify myself to teach writing and editing to Nigerian nationals. Then in 1961, I was invited by the University of Nigeria at Nsukka to teach in its Jackson College of Journalism, the first degree-granting journalism school of its kind in English-speaking West Africa.

Serving as Jackson's acting head and initially as its only faculty member, I worked under the close supervision of Dr. Nnamdi Azikiwe—then chancellor of the university, owner of Nigeria's largest chain of newspapers, and also the nation's first president—to launch the journalism college. I was privileged to teach there for several years, until the outbreak of the Nigerian Civil War in 1967 and my subsequent repatriation in 1970 brought that service opportunity to an end for me.

During my years at Nsukka, the students confirmed what Jim Johnson had already proved—*no one communicates with a people better than one of their own.*

Go and learn what this means:
The writer is the servant of his audience.

3
Teacher and Mentor

Daniel V. Runyon

Dan Runyon attended Wheaton Graduate School from 1976-78
specifically to study fiction writing and magazine editing
from Jim Johnson. He has coauthored eight books, and
hundreds of his articles have been published. He is editor of
The Missionary Tidings, the world mission news magazine
of the Free Methodist Church, and lives with his wife and
three children in rural Michigan.

*M*ail Pouch Tobacco was known to advertise on barns in this rural community in the Upper Peninsula of Michigan. Young Jim Johnson figured he could advertise in the same way. Still, he was expecting a spanking—or worse —when his father came home wondering who painted the "editorial" on the end of the barn.

A major community fiasco was coming to a head. Whether it had to do with the local parson, the fire chief, or the mayor was of no consequence. What concerned the elder Johnson was the absence of a signature on the barn graffiti. Only a yellow-bellied coward would do such a thing.

"If you wrote it, you sign it," was the fatherly concern of Jim's dad. So poor Jim had to get out the paint and a ladder, climb up there in broad daylight, and scrawl his "John Hancock" to the opinions so blatantly plastered to the barn. Johnson learned at an early age the valuable lesson of accountability.

He told this childhood story to virtually every would-be writer to cross his path in future decades.

I was a shy youngster who broke into journalism by publishing *The Spy,* an anonymous, underground, college campus monthly newsletter. Between the time the dining hall was unlocked in the morning and well before breakfast, I furtively circulated the clandestine journalism by placing half-a-dozen copies at each table, then slinking back to the dorm for a shower, followed by a leisurely walk to the cafeteria for a nice literary "surprise." So covert were my operations that in two years of activity even my roommate had no clue to the origins of *The Spy.*

Jim Johnson's lesson on accountability was not lost on me. Every student of Jim's had to accept full responsibility for whatever he or she wrote. Johnson made sure of this by copying our homework onto transparencies and shining them on the wall for the class to evaluate. Word by word, sentence by sentence, we picked apart our work, demonstrating over and over again that the first draft is never the best possible writing.

I once objected to this nitpicky business by reminding our professor that C. S. Lewis was rumored to have written *The Chronicles of Narnia* in longhand, then shipping them off to the printer with little more than a glance back over his work.

"When you write as well as C. S. Lewis, I invite you to do the same," was Johnson's reply. Then, throwing my literary acumen on the wall using his trusty overhead projector, with a few deft strokes of that black felt marker, Jim illustrated to the entire class several ways in which my work might be improved.

In 1976 at the Wheaton College Graduate School there was no Billy Graham Center. Writing classes were held up the stairs and to the left in humble Buswell Hall. There gathered a mere handful of six or eight students in a faded room reminiscent of prints in history books of colonial America. Forget about computers, desktop publishing, and laser printers. Picture tile floors, wooden desks, ink wells, and black and white images of Ben Franklin and Noah Webster.

The beam from Jim Johnson's overhead projector slashed through this pastoral scene like the headlight of a heavily loaded freight train. There on the wall is your sentence, and Jim is saying . . .

"'Slashed?' Are you sure 'slashed' is the word you want here? Do overhead projectors 'slash'? How about 'dissected,' or maybe 'pierced'? 'Sliced'? And, are you sure the train analogy adds anything to the image? Maybe it detracts? Does your reader have experience with trains? Is this a natural parallel or are you just groping for more words to fill up the assignment? Who is your audience? What is it you're really trying to say here?"

You mumble, "Well, the point is that modern technology is beginning to revolutionize the training of writers—and we want the reader to feel the same vulnerability we feel, sitting here with you dicing up our work like so many potatoes . . ."

Jim Johnson didn't just grade papers, he edited them. Writing for him was always a challenge. Anticipating how he would react was always a puzzle. It took me the better part of a year to feel as though I had him figured out.

Right off the bat (yes, Jim, this particular cliché is precisely what I want to use here), right off the bat Jim made me mad (yes, "mad" like a dog, not "angry" like a housewife), so I dug in my heels and fought back. "Take that, and that, and that!" I yelled at my portable Adler typewriter each time I punched in a sentence I thought might make it past the critical gaze of "ole Jim."

He threw down the gauntlet early in my career at Wheaton by slapping a B- grade on a perfect masterpiece. Following his evaluation, I gathered up the pieces and rewrote more to Johnson's liking. So he relabeled it with a B + along with a notation that to get an A I needed to demonstrate original thinking!

One day a particularly excellent article I wrote was shining on the wall in Buswell Hall, the name covered up to encourage honesty on the part of student editors. "This is great stuff!" exhorted a colleague, but Johnson hushed him right up with an admonition to "Watch it—we can't let it go to his head."

In fairness, Johnson did parcel out praise in just the right amounts, whenever needed for motivational purposes. Like a mechanic who knows both how to keep a clunker on the road and how to fine-tune a Mercedes, Jim seemed to know the standard by which each student should be judged and equipped. The broken reed he would not break.

Jim's other saving grace was his lousy ability at math. In that first fiction writing class he gave me one "B" after another on the homework assignments, but the final grade on my report card turned up an A-. When you come to understand this system of grading, then you have come to understand our beloved writing professor, James L. Johnson.

It was easy to picture Johnson in the military or as an editor. Seeing his human side came as a greater challenge, so I was delighted when he invited us to have class in his living room one evening. His wife was there. His son ducked through briefly. His dog lollygagged around in the living room. Here was a human being with a family.

Jim even showed us the basement office where novels that got published were written. He pointed out the laundry chute through which he once escaped after asking Rosemary to lock him in so he could meet some deadlines. He signed a few copies of his books and judiciously meted them out to deserving, soon-to-be-graduates. He offered us a bit of refreshment.

Back in class, it was fellow student Sandy Majorowicz who brought to my attention that all was not well with Jim. In my adversarial role I came to class always ready for battle, but Sandy seemed to detect that Jim was a bit green around the gills. She saw the cold sweat. She detected the way he fought to keep his feet, standing there behind that heavy wood desk. She sensed when his jaw was clenched in a fight with pain. She heard his pounding chest half a room away.

"That man should be in the hospital," Sandy said one day. But he kept coming to class, up that long stairway, a stack of freshly graded papers (and the ever present transparencies) tucked under one arm. Quite often he wore a white, short-sleeved shirt. Beads of moisture stood out on those bare arms as he held forth in front of class trying not to let on to any sign of pain or fatigue. He was macho. I was pretty sure he would tough it out.

Some years later I developed a theory on why Jim projected such bravado. I read *Before Honor,* in which Johnson relates the horror of Navy Captain Eugene B. McDaniel's six years of suffering as a prisoner of war at the hands of Viet Cong. McDaniel's physical and mental torture is graphically communicated. Johnson seems to be vicariously experiencing the pain of the POW. The book was published in 1975, and Johnson was my teacher in 1976. The parallels in that story and my experience with Jim are striking. Two examples:

McDaniel, the POW, finds a limited freedom as a result of tampering with and sneaking through a vent on the ceiling of his prison cell. Johnson, the author, attempts a similar escape from the prison of his office via the laundry chute.

On a bombing run deep in enemy territory, McDaniel, the soon-to-be POW, ejects at the last possible moment from his disintegrating A-6 Intruder aircraft mangled from the explosion of a surface to air missile (SAM). In the classroom is Johnson, prisoner in a body of flesh with a heart that misfires. But he is flying over enemy territory, pushing his "machinery" to the limit and will wait for the last possible moment to eject.

POW McDaniel found he had to communicate or die. He risked his life for the most inconsequential tidbits of information. Johnson was equally compelled—communicate or die —a calling for every Christian. No wonder Jim's classes seemed to me like a war zone.

More than a teacher Johnson was a man with a mission. My first clue to this came a month or so after my arrival at Wheaton. My goal in life was to become a novelist, a writer of great works of fiction while collecting handsome royalties. Like James Michener, I would travel to exotic places, sit by the fire at evening and scrawl out literary masterpieces, and occasionally reward my publisher with thick packets of mail causing him to tremble with excitement as he personally wrote out yet another big check as the meager reward for my brilliance.

Thus inspired, I called the graduate school to make an appointment with Jim Johnson. To my surprise, he had no office at the graduate school but maintained digs at a place called Evangelical Literature Overseas (ELO). I called the number, made an appointment, and some days later found myself climbing a narrow stairway, turning right, pushing open a door, and confronting Nancy, the part-time ELO secretary. "Have a seat," she said. "He'll be with you shortly."

These were cramped quarters. Things were stacked in piles. There seemed to be just this waiting area and a room behind it. I could hear Johnson's voice on the telephone, his voice carrying the tone more of barking orders than offering fatherly advice. The place seemed to be more of a mission outpost than the corporate offices of an influential literary genius.

I should have paid closer attention in class that day when Jim talked about his stint with that missions magazine in Africa. He had carried on about the challenges of cross-cultural communication, the dangers of mediocrity and complacency, and the need to take risks for the sake of the kingdom. When our attention lagged, he cajoled us with pictures he personally took of Richard Nixon in Africa long before the world would recognize him as either Mr. President or Tricky Dick.

Jim was still on the telephone, so my thoughts harked back to the summer previous when I attended the *Decision*

Magazine School for Christian Writers in Minneapolis. Already accepted for admission to Wheaton College Graduate School, I thought some preliminary studies would be in order, and they were. In Minneapolis I attended seminars conducted by Sherwood Wirt, Jim Johnson, and Victor Oliver, an eloquent speaker with his own Viet Nam stories and who would later teach a class I took in cross-cultural communications. All of those men challenged me to a deeper commitment to Jesus Christ and a resolve to use my gifts to advance His kingdom.

So I had already heard a few of Johnson's "sermons." Up here in this ELO office I was about to see him practice what he preached. The telephone voice was no longer coming through the door. The secretary warned Jim that a student with an appointment was here to see him. A moment later the door hinged open, and I was invited into the inner sanctum.

Alone in the presence of the man who would endow me with his literary gift, I fumbled for words. Finally, it came out that I had one motive in attending Wheaton College Graduate School—to learn all I could about fiction writing from Jim Johnson. I would take all his classes as well as independent studies; I would type relentlessly, revise continually until all was excellence. I even imagined myself traveling to the ends of the earth on special assignment for Jim, conducting research for the next Code Name Sebastian novel.

Well, it didn't work out. In the first place, my motives to achieve comfort, leisure, fame, and success as a writer suddenly seemed out of place—even sinful. In the second place, Johnson advised me that I could never succeed with my dream. Even if I was a better writer than Steinbeck or more connected than Updike, forget it. For every Christian writer who makes it big, thousands never sell an article.

Jim put it to me straight. To succeed as a writer, one thing is necessary—discipline. You must write every *day*. You must write every *way*—news, obituaries, interviews, features, editorials, essays, short stories, cereal box hype, advertising copy. A good carpenter is one who had learned to drive any sort of nail, and a good writer is one who had learned to produce any sort of literature. If that was what I wanted to learn, then Jim would be happy to teach me. Otherwise, I might as well pack my bags.

"Nobody likes to write," I was advised. "We like to *have written.*" To be an "instant" success requires ten, twenty, or thirty years—maybe a lifetime—of hard work. Go and learn what this means: the writer is the servant of his audience.

What an interview! I escaped with my life and little else save the resolve to stand up to this ego-basher for the duration of graduate school. But everything Jim told me proved true with the exception of one comment that may have been a joke to begin with: "Nobody likes to write—we just like to *have written.*" I loved to write and still do. The first draft is a creative adventure, the multitude of revisions thereafter a delicate and redemptive surgery.

Upon graduation I took Jim's advice about the need to write every day and took the first job offered to me, "scut work" journalism. It promised little besides food on the table and mandatory time each day at the typewriter.

Psalm 116:15 claims, "Precious in the sight of the Lord is the death of his saints." For many years I could not understand the verse, perhaps because I didn't know many saints who had died. Reading commentaries on this passage left me disillusioned; some claimed "precious" means costly, indicating that the life of the saint is valuable. No doubt about that. Losing a leader like Jim Johnson would leave a gaping hole in the ranks. Yet, there must be a deeper meaning.

The news flash went out—Jim had had another heart attack, this one fatal. Multitudes grieved, a funeral was planned, and I asked my wife, who had never met Jim, to drop everything for a day. We made the long trip from our home in Michigan back to the Cliff Barrows Auditorium in the Billy Graham Center at Wheaton for a final tribute to this towering spiritual and literary giant.

Farmland and fruit orchards flashed by the window as we drove. I told Renée my best Jim Johnson stories and, oddly, thought about farmers harvesting crops. When the grain is ripe (and not a day before), they gather it into their barns. When the fruit is plump and luscious, it is picked. Precious in the sight of the farmer is the harvesting of his crops.

It was a moving memorial service that Sunday. We who remained, still too tough and green to be of much use in heaven, offered condolences to Jim's family and praise for our esteemed colleague and mentor. Today we live not in his shadow, but in the light of his image.

He believed that most Christian novels were not merely fictitious, but dangerously untrue.

4
The Novelist

Jerry B. Jenkins

A full-time writer and writer-in-residence at the Moody
Bible Institute, Jerry Jenkins is a prolific author of books,
including biographies, novels, and nonfiction, and has
written articles for dozens of magazines. Through Jim Johnson,
he became a visiting journalism lecturer at Wheaton College
Graduate School. Recently he undertook a journalism teaching
assignment at Daystar University College in Nairobi, Kenya,
for Media Associates International, Inc. Jerry, his wife,
and three sons live near Zion, Illinois.

*W*e met at a writer's conference, I more than twenty years his junior and intimidated by this gruff, macho, fast-talking man. He was stern, opinionated, even cynical. But as we continued to chat over the years at various conferences and seminars, I gradually learned the truth that so many before me had learned. The exterior was phony! James L. Johnson was a pussycat, a soft-hearted, emotional man who cared deeply for the individual.

Eventually, he asked me to substitute teach for him occasionally at the Wheaton Graduate School. "I have no degrees," I told him. "The students will see right through me."

He scowled. "You're editor of *Moody Monthly,* and you can write," he grumbled. "If there's one thing we don't need more of, it's unpublished, pedigreed profs."

Jim asked me to teach a semester for him while he went to Africa. I was thrilled, honored, humbled—the latter when a call came from someone at the grad school. "We have all the information we need except your years of postgraduate education."

"That," I said, "makes an inaccurate assumption." There could be no postgraduate work if there was no graduation.

"I see. Well, there is the matter of our trying to maintain a high average number of years of postgraduate education among our staff." The man was deeply concerned that though I had a couple of years of college, I had not even an associate of arts degree. "I'll get back to you," he said.

I called Jim saying I appreciated his confidence, predicting that I would not be approved to teach an entire semester.

"Bureaucrats!" he spat. "He'll get back to you all right. Start planning your syllabus."

I never asked him what he said or to whom, but he paved the way for me to teach several graduate courses, as he had paved the way for Christian novelists. His fiction became unique because it penetrated to the general reader market.

His first four novels, those with the marvelous titles, allowed a Christian lead character to be dynamic, action oriented, imperfect, and exciting.

Code Name Sebastian (Lippincott, 1967)
The Nine Lives of Alphonse (Lippincott, 1968)
A Handful of Dominoes (Lippincott, 1970)
A Piece of the Moon Is Missing (Lippincott/Holman, 1974)

I read those four eagerly—plus *Trackless Seas* (Crossway, 1987), published shortly before he died—and have attempted to emulate Jim in that genre.

It was difficult at times to separate the man from the novelist, indeed even the man from his title character. Jim did not hesitate to wear his faith, or his lack of it, on his sleeve. If he was struggling spiritually, or at least battling some cosmic questions, people knew it. He loved the search, the journey, the quest. If his brazen, outspoken doubts made you uncomfortable, so much the better. If he had to suffer doubts and fear and confusion in his spiritual walk, why shouldn't you? If you have answers, he'd imply, let's hear them. If you don't, quit pretending everything is rosy.

Balancing his curmudgeon act was a deadly sense of humor. You eventually saw the twinkle in his eye and realized he was putting you on. He was not angry, not frustrated. He was having fun. He would call me at the office and tell my secretary, "No names. Tell him it's the CIA."

The next time he identified himself as one of *my* lead characters.

Once he said he was Henry Kissinger.

Then I got a legitimate call from the White House. My secretary said, "Mr. Johnson, is that you?"

The beauty of Ray Sebastian was that he was imperfect and struggling. *Code Name Sebastian*, the flagship novel of the series, begins with the title character in spiritual doldrums. When the commercial jet he's on crashes in the Negev Desert, it is only fitting, for his "forty years" in spiritual desolation have just begun.

Jim made Sebastian a reluctant hero, a man of action because he had to be. Rather than a tough-as-nails private eye or a world-wise international agent, Sebastian was a young widower, a pastor in desperate need of a touch from God. The novelist in Jim plunged his hero into impossible circumstances and let him work his way through and out of them. No miracles, no overt divine intervention, no clichés.

Better yet, Jim sold the books to the secular market. He had talked long and often about the need to take a credible Christian witness into the mainstream of life. He had been trying to do that throughout his career as a pastor, a missionary, and an educator. He sent a batch of pages to an editor in New York and was stunned to receive a check for a thousand dollars and a contract.

Writer's conference audiences all over the world have laughed with him as he recounts those heady, giddy days. All of a sudden, with success, a green light, and the encouragement of not just money but also moral support from the real world, he couldn't write.

He rearranged the furniture in his office, bought new gadgets, a sound system, new music. Nothing worked till the deadline approached. Then he hammered away, beating the plot line into submission, forcing his characters in and out of each others' lives until the story took shape.

Jim wasn't afraid to be honest about a man and a woman. He wasn't afraid to present to the secular market a Christian who was imperfect, who had questions, who struggled with his faith. "Don't ever," he warned writers, "be afraid of truth with a capital T." He believed that most Christian novels were not merely fictitious, but dangerously untrue.

"If we can't stomach them, how can we expect the unbelieving world to bother?"

I had written nothing of book length when I first discovered the Sebastian books, and for the next few years I wrote only nonfiction. But when asked to try my hand at fiction, I began carefully with a mystery series, U.S.-based. The first person I sent a published copy to was Jim Johnson. He was as easy to draw a compliment from as a phone solicitor is to get rid of.

"Fun," he said. "Broaden your horizons."

He said it as if I should know precisely what he was talking about, so I didn't dare ask him to elaborate. Often, when asked to be more specific, Jim only repeated his first pronouncement. A friend of mine, new in the business, sent his first fiction manuscript to Jim, hoping for a reaction.

Several months passed, then the manuscript was returned with a scribbled note. "It's publishable. J. J."

My friend was disappointed and put the thing away for weeks before asking me to read it. I didn't want to, didn't have the time, didn't know how to say no. "Has anyone else seen it?" I asked.

"Jim Johnson."

I just knew Jim would have told him the truth. "What'd he say?"

"Not much. Just that it was publishable."

It was difficult to explain to him that when Jim Johnson said something was publishable, that was like getting a ticker tape parade from a librarian. I eagerly read the book. It absorbed me. It was published.

Meanwhile, I kept shoving my published mystery series offerings Jim's way.

"Lots of fun," he'd say. "Take your imagination overseas and watch your themes expand."

Thanks, Jim. Man, that guy could be obtuse.

Finally, I did it. An editor said the same thing Jim had been saying. Take more chances. Broaden. Expand. Be more ambitious. "When you can do these little books in your sleep," Jim said, "it's time to do a big one."

I followed Jim into international espionage thriller territory with *The Operative* (Harper & Row) in 1987. His effusive response? "What'd I tell you? I knew you could do it."

That meant he liked it, and I knew that was all I'd get. It was enough. I'd heard him tell the truth enough times to know that he would not sit still for a less-than-best effort, friend or not.

His *The Death of Kings* is my favorite of all his fiction. It was written for Doubleday (1974) and, though it is not part of the Sebastian series, it remains, in my mind, his most ambitious and successful work. Layered, textured, heavily researched, gritty, earthy, complete in itself—it was his masterpiece.

The story is set mainly in Africa, and reading it is one of those magical experiences that transports you immediately to another place, another continent, another culture. In the pages of that novel, I was there. I wouldn't actually visit Africa until 1989; but when I did, I knew precisely where the déjà vu came from.

As I've matured, particularly as a reader, I find myself harder and harder to please. I give books only a certain number of pages to grab me. I want a book that pulls me back, that makes me want to read it even when I should be doing other things. Then I talk myself into waiting until my daily private reading time, and the experience is all that much more fun.

The Death of Kings is that kind of book. When was the last time you read a big book more than once? *The Death* is the kind you read again as soon as you finish it the first time. Then a year or two later, you read it again.

The characters were dead on, brash, young pilots. Some were privileged and spoiled, some devout, some crazy. Mission executives, lifelong "servants," were people I could almost recognize. Description, dialogue, the appeal to my senses, it was all there.

You'll find *The Death of Kings* only in certain libraries now, but it's worth the search. Within its pages—as in the Sebastian series—you'll find the man I miss, the one who opened the door for crossover Christian fiction into the secular market. Jim's alter ego is in these books; when I read selected passages, I can hear him and see him in more than one character.

I miss him, and though it raises a lump in my throat, I enjoy the sweet memory of the reading of his last piece of writing at his memorial service in Barrows Auditorium, Wheaton College Graduate School. He had some premonition of his death, and he bade farewell on paper. The years have dulled the details of it all, save for the precious line "I'll see you at the eastern gate."

How I look forward to that.

I never again thought of him as average—in any way.

5
Master Motivator

Donald R. Brown

Donald R. Brown became director of the Office of Information of
the National Association of Evangelicals (NAE) in 1984 and is
editor of NAE's journal, *United Evangelical ACTION*.
The author (or coauthor) of five books, he has been selling
articles and short stories for almost thirty years.
He traces his earliest motivation to write professionally
to Jim Johnson's influence.

*A*t first, he looked—well, he looked rather *average!*
Perhaps a bit taller than the norm, but by no means a tall
man. His hair was dark, yet not distinctively black. As a matter of fact, there wasn't anything particularly distinctive about
him—at first. But soon, he proved quite special. I never again
thought of him as average—in any way.

He walked about the front of the classroom, energetically,
then sat nervously on a chair. After a moment or two, he
looked out the dirty, sixth-floor window, down at the busy
Chicago city streets. From time to time, he glanced at us, his
audience, as we stirred, attempting to guess what he was doing.

The thirty-plus writer's conference attendees and I were
puzzled: after what seemed a long time—actually less than
five minutes—the man finally spoke.

That pseudo gruff voice growled, "OK. Now, for the next
few minutes write a description of what I've been doing—and
why!"

He locked eyes with many of us, and the corners of his
mouth quivered just before he broke into his brief but infec-
tious grin.

That was my introduction to James L. Johnson at a Christian Life Writer's Conference held at Moody Bible Institute in the early sixties.

I suppose we won't know until we get to heaven how many people Jim affected at such conferences and seminars. I heard him at several different gatherings, but no other session remains as indelible on my mind as that first time. Those two or three days were unique for me; the director of the conference, a Moody student, Jim, and I were the only males attending all the sessions. The other three dozen conferees were women.

Jim was sometimes accused of inventing the phrase, "little old ladies in tennis shoes," referring to a number of the attendees at many writer's conferences. If he did coin the phrase, it was not intended to be derogatory or insulting—it was simply an objective observation and accurate reporting. At that first conference, I noted that Jim was hounded by several diminutive, elderly women who literally wore tennis shoes —sneakers (long before the day of Nike and Adidas)—and carried stacks of poems and other manuscripts.

He attracted crowds after each session because he was both magnetic and polite. After answering the same questions many times, he exasperatedly began one session by saying, "Let me answer several questions that are *always* asked." He then recited a litany of "Yes, you *always* send a SASE with your manuscript." "How long should your article be? *Long enough* to tell your story!" and a number of similar admonitions.

I wish I could remember exactly what he said in those days that motivated me to continue trying to write. I eventually sold my first article and have been writing—and selling what I write—ever since. Other individuals have had a part in the training, evaluation, encouragement, and motivations that have kept me going, obviously. But no one individual has been more influential to this writer than Jim. Sadly, I'm not sure I ever told him that.

Jim somehow knew intuitively who needed to be cajoled, who needed to be encouraged. He could always deter-
mine what needed to be said in certain situations for each
individual. He sensed when to challenge, when to comfort,
when to push, and when to back off. No, that's inaccurate;
Jim *never* "backed off." Perhaps he sometimes "let up."

Jim often complained that mission organizations only
partially completed their task. He would dramatically tell
how many missionaries dedicated their entire careers—their
lives—to reducing a tribe's language to writing, translating
large portions of the Bible into that language and eventually
teaching the people of the area to read. "But," he would rave,
"what did the mission organizations give the nationals to
read besides the Bible? *Nothing!*—unless it was a few hymns."

Then he'd look at his listeners. "But the Communists
and the Muslims gave them plenty of stuff to read."

Jim's strong convictions about such a situation were
certainly part of the impetus for his involvement with Evangelical Literature Overseas. He was keenly aware of the need
for newly literate Christians in other lands to have more than
the Bible to read.

When he was on the platform, Jim poured himself into
all those who would open themselves to him. The audience
could be an entire conference, or a small class, or even one
individual; the number made no difference. He worked as
hard to inspire one as one hundred.

I had the rare privilege of sitting over coffee with Jim
and Wilbert Norton (see chap. 11) during some of their early
conversations about initiating a graduate program in communications at the Wheaton College Graduate School. By then, I
was editor of *Wheaton Alumni* magazine.

I marveled at the vision Jim and Dr. Norton shared, pursued, and finally brought to fruition. They overcame a mountain of obstacles to initiate a fledgling graduate communications program that has grown in size and prestige.

Today, hundreds of alums of that program are aiding the entire Christian mission effort around the world.

Although he was the chief catalyst behind this successful communications program, Jim characteristically claimed no personal glory; he gave any accolades to his Lord.

At another writers' conference at Green Lake, Wisconsin, I became better acquainted with Jim. He wasn't present, but I met *Code Name Sebastian.* I purchased the novel, walked to the beautiful lakefront, found a chair in the shade, and sat down to read the first chapter. However, I didn't stir from that chair until I had read the entire book. Talk about a "page turner"!

Over the years, I had the privilege of getting more personally acquainted with Jim. He was directing Evangelical Literature Overseas and had offices in the *Christian Life* magazine's building in Carol Stream. That was in the sixties, when I was a part-time CWI (Christian Writer's Institute, a correspondence school) instructor and occasionally conferred with Jim about specific, difficult problems raised by a particular student's response to the course assignment.

During those years I also enrolled in the communications program at the Wheaton Graduate School. In the 1971-72 school year, I reveled in a fiction writing course taught by Jim.

I specifically recall a number of his verbal gems in those days. One suggestion he made in a particular case eighteen years ago I still follow faithfully today as I try to complete a novel. The class session began with typical administrative necessities and a moment of banter between Jim and various students. Then he squared his jaw and shoulders and thundered. "How do you get your characters to sound like real people? You create your characters, then put them into a tension filled situation, and *write down what you hear them say to each other!*"

I sat without taking notes for a moment, uncertain if I had heard him correctly. "Could you repeat that statement, please?" I requested.

He smiled, almost. He nodded slightly with his typical loving/indulgent expression so common when challenged. He moved across the front of the little classroom with a gait that somehow hinted at a combination of marching, prancing, and/or strutting. He moved his head in a bit of a herky-jerky movement as if slightly agitated but still with a distinctive twinkle in his eye. "Brown, you heard what I said—you just don't believe it works."

He was right—I didn't believe it then, but it does work. When I write fiction, I sometimes look back at a piece of dialogue and wonder where it came from. Then I realize that I have simply been writing down what I heard my characters say to each other in that particular situation! Jim, if he were still living, wouldn't be at all surprised. After all, he told me twice.

During the final few years of his life, I had the privilege of working in the same building with Jim. He was associate executive director of resource development for World Relief of NAE. Occasionally, he encouraged me for something he liked in an issue of *United Evangelical Action;* at other times, he gently chided me for not getting wider coverage for an important NAE event. More often, he shared his concern for some problem within the Christian family—close to home or on the other side of the globe.

He had a detailed grasp of many world problems yet saw the very human needs of those who worked around him. He was farsighted about the needs of the church around the world, but his human bifocals remained sharp.

All too rarely, he allowed himself to be drafted to give the devotional thought in our weekly chapel service. His reflections usually provided new and creative insights into God's Word and/or a unique glimpse at the way God was working through some individual's life.

His brief verbal presentations were laced with his wry humor, but he was never the comedian; he always spoke with "thus saith the Lord" but never paraded himself as an authority. I miss his standing at the speaker's stand, as his perceptive eyes panned the room; the corners of his eyes seemed somehow connected to the corresponding corners of his mouth as that small smile threatened to explode all over his face. His lower lip protruded ever so slightly—I was never certain if it was his tongue pushing against the lip or if it was just an extension of his determined jaw.

When he began speaking, his logic and creative thoughts became a connection between himself and his audience—each of us seemed to experience, not just see, his meaningful and energetic gestures. A rare person—he communicated verbally as effectively as in print.

Jim drove himself excessively, accomplishing more than one man should. He worked hard at whatever "regular job" was at hand then wrote long hours at night and other times that were "his own." I feel intimidated when I see his accomplishment of writing sixteen books (all excellent quality writing) and realize how long I've been working on a single novel.

Jim's final position with World Relief included fund-raising (see chap. 12, by Marlene Minor). I always understood he did a superb job. He put all his efforts and creativity to work on raising the funds. He once commented that "we have to get to that relatively small pool of resources first, using the best story and with the most effective request." He wanted desperately to find new, untapped sources of funds whether that proved to be people with a lot of money no one else knew about or foundations that weren't being inundated by proposals from every other evangelical organization.

I have always believed that a lack of an earned doctorate stood between Jim and the proper respect due him from the academic community. Or perhaps it was the lack of the degree coupled with the fact that he wrote *adventure* fiction. I believe he could have earned as many degrees as he wished; he simply chose to use his talents and energies in different spheres.

Jim was a master communicator, but his genius was seldom appreciated or recognized. The book *Hunt for Red October* and the financially successful movie by the same name were less exciting than (and not nearly as creative, in my opinion) Jim's final Sebastian novel, *Trackless Seas*. I am mystified why someone has not made a motion picture or a TV series based on the Sebastian stories. All the ingredients are there: interesting characters, exciting episodes, worldwide locations, up-to-date intrigue. Screenwriters and Hollywood agents should be standing in line for the rights to Sebastian.

I am even more mystified why the Sebastian stories never caught on with the Christian public and never were heralded by the evangelical media, especially when I see Frank Peretti's fiction selling millions of copies.

It is sad that no institution of Christian higher education ever conferred an L.L.D. or some other honorary degree on Jim. Perhaps "Dr. Johnson" wouldn't have been an appropriate title for the bright, clear thinking, plain speaking, humble servant of God who had no hesitation to "call a spade a shovel." Jim's early death brought large numbers of people together for his memorial service on June 28, 1987. He had prepared an order of service for such an eventuality. And quite properly, there was a platform full of people praising and eulogizing Jim. But to me, it was a bit late for some of the praise. He should have been formally honored in many ways years before his home-going.

The day before Jim died he came downstairs from his World Relief (WRC) office and made the round of all the offices at the National Association of Evangelicals. He occasionally made visits but usually was quite busy and always in a rush. On that particular day, however, he seemed relaxed and unhurried. He seemed to be touching all the bases, giving all of us one last pleasant memory. Perhaps he had a premonition; possibly his movements were prompted by the Holy Spirit.

He appeared quite healthy—the contacts seemed perfectly normal. On previous forays he had been pleasantly caustic, if such an oxymoron is possible. More than anyone else I knew, he sensed which persons responded to a verbal caress and who needed a vocal karate chop. He was both gifted and sensitive to the gift.

After his death some said, "If he could have driven himself a little less . . . if he could have felt less frustration about things over which he had no control . . . if he could have assumed a little less personal responsibility for raising WRC funds . . ."

There are always a lot of "ifs," "maybes," and "perhapses," but then that would have been someone else, not Jim Johnson.

Even Jim identified himself as a "Type A" personality. He was driven and determined, active and aggressive; he was indeed an energetic workaholic. Moreover, he was constantly and compulsively striving for more, for better. But Jim was far more than a "Type A" personality. He was an "A Plus" person.

The world is richer for his mountain of contributions. We who knew and loved him have enhanced lives because of all he gave us.

Jim was more of a topical speaker than an expository preacher. . . . His messages were animated, peppered with anecdotes.

6
Innovative Pastor

Herbert and Phyllis Bailey

Herb and Phyllis Bailey, graduates of Moody Bible Institute,
have been friends of Jim and Rosemary Johnson for more than
thirty years. The two couples met at Moody where Jim was
studying while pastoring at Elm-LaSalle Bible Church. Herb,
an employee of Moody for more than thirty years,is
assistant production manager for manufacturing at Moody Press,
Chicago. Phyllis is employed at Elmhurst Memorial Hospital
in the dietary department. They reside in Elmhurst, Illinois.

*P*hyllis and Herb Bailey. LaVerne Shaw. Pop
Mitchell. Travis Bentley. Dewey Daniels. Madge Vanderwater.
Madge's daughter and church organist Edna Olmstead. Dick
Reid. Alice Baugess. They and the Vernon Anthony family
were among the people that Jim Johnson faced every Sunday
morning. They were the core of the congregation of the Elm-
LaSalle Bible Church that Jim pastored from 1959-61.

He had been chosen to be the pastor by Moody Memorial Church, the governing body of Elm-LaSalle Bible Church in
those days. Jim plunged into the work at the church. His enthusiasm caught on. He was an encourager. As we recall,
Dick Reid came on staff as youth director. Omar Reese came
on as song leader. Jim supported the Billy Graham rallies
held in Chicago. He got parishioners out to distribute flyers
in the run-down tenements and dilapidated housing units in
the neighborhood. Jim was faithful to his little flock, nurturing them through Bible teaching and visiting them when they
were in trouble.

Jim was more of a topical speaker than an expository
preacher, and he moved around a lot when he preached. His

messages were very animated, peppered with anecdotes of his navy days and his childhood days in the Upper Peninsula of Michigan in a little town called Dollar Bay.

At Elm-LaSalle, Jim served a cross-section of the Near North Side population of Chicago. He ministered to the down-and-outers as well as the forerunners of the yuppie generation and a few professional people. One poorly dressed old lady came regularly into the morning worship service (she would be called a bag lady today) carrying a brown paper bag. During the service, she'd pull a handful of roast beef from the lunch bag and munch it during the service. She alternated with a handful of chocolate creams from another bag she carried. Some were annoyed and offended. Remarking on it later, Jim said, "This is what the church is all about—to serve all types of people."

I was introduced to Jim by my wife, Phyllis, at Elm-LaSalle Church. I went to hear Jim speak at her urging. Like many Moody Bible Institute (MBI) students, I usually attended Moody Church, but after hearing Jim at Elm-LaSalle, I attended there. Many other students followed, and the church, which had undergone a slump in attendance, started growing again. Under Jim Johnson the church began carrying its weight financially as attendance grew. We believe giving increased because Jim introduced the people to the Lord Jesus Christ and His Word in such a way that they fell in love with Him and supported the ministry that meant so much to them.

Jim got individuals involved. Like the gentleman who faithfully drove his car over to the Cabrini-Green housing project, just west of the church, to pick up the African-American youngsters after school for Bible classes at the church. Then there was Agnes McDaniels from Kentucky, whose smile and brimming heart of love bespoke the indwelling of the Holy Spirit as she wrapped her arms around the little kids in her Sunday school class. Seeds that were sown then later developed into concrete programs under Jim's successor, Bill Leslie.

Jim was not one to fall into lockstep with a particular mind-set. His work as a missionary to Nigeria contributed to his openness to new ideas. His friendliness brought MBI students because he related to them as adults. He could identify with them because he also sat in the classroom with them, albeit slightly older than most of them. Students liked Jim.

Though Jim debated vigorously with minds sharper than his, and held his own in discussing concepts and theories, he never talked down to people. He treated us as though we were on the same level. Although we knew we were not, he made us feel that we were, and we loved him for that.

Jim enjoyed telling a story. Many had a wry twist to them. Jim recounted an incident. One day, while sitting in the church office, two men in black overcoats came in and asked if he was the preacher. "Yes," Jim said. Convinced, they quickly "persuaded" him to accompany them to a funeral parlor on North Avenue. In the room was a pine casket. "Read over him," they said. Jim read a Bible passage.

Immediately the men marched him to the door, slipped him a twenty dollar bill, saying, "That's it!" Jim smiled about the incident because he later learned that the mortuary was a Chicago mob hangout.

Phyllis first met Jim in the apologetics class at Moody Bible Institute. She remembers his sitting in the back row slouched down in his seat with his knee pressing up against the seat ahead of him. Jim didn't contribute a great deal to the class discussion. However, the professor, Mr. Dunnett, graded on the curve, and the entire class was affected by one person's high grades—Jim Johnson's.

Little did we realize that this man, who one day would sit on the platform with great evangelical leaders such as Billy Graham and make an unprecedented contribution to Christian writing through his many writings, books, and leadership at ELO, was to become such a blessing as we got to know him and Rosemary.

Jim and Rosemary always made us feel at home with them. Even later, when their circle of friends grew to include professional people, professors, doctors, and authors, they never failed to include the Baileys, whom they had known and loved since Elm-LaSalle Church days. That's the kind of friend Jim was.

Long after he left Elm-LaSalle, Jim labored on behalf of the church:

- he urged the church to open a Christian bookstore nearby to reach disillusioned young people, many of whom had been influenced in one way or another by the Jesus Movement
- he brought in funding for outreach programs and the planning of a moderate income housing development involving several neighborhood churches
- he found money to pay for a computerized survey of the congregation's beliefs and identity as well as opinions on issues confronting Christianity and society

Since his years at Elm-LaSalle Bible Church Jim Johnson has influenced thousands through his books. Yet the congregation of common folk from Elm-LaSalle still feel the impact Jim made on their lives for good and for God. Jim rose to prominence in the evangelical world and traveled far and wide from the modest gothic church on LaSalle Street. But the interlude at Elm-LaSalle between missionary service in Nigeria and his careers as author, professor, and speaker, helped to forge Jim's vision for a lost world and the desire to reach men and women for Christ through Christian literature.

*His letters read as though he were
out of breath and running to catch the
last train out of town. In spite of this, he
always managed to nail his basic premise.*

7
Through an Editor's Eyes

Judith E. Markham

Judith E. Markham has spent twenty-eight years as an editor in
religious publishing. She is a partner/owner of Blue Water Ink,
a book production company in Grand Rapids, Michigan, where
she spends her time writing, editing, reading, and trying to
understand her computer. Judith has led three editorial
workshops (one for Spanish editors) for Media Associates
International, Inc. She and her husband live in Cascade, Michigan.

What does a man of God do when faced with the harsh
realities of being in the world, relating to the world? What does a
man of God do when there are no easy solutions to problems,
no simple prayers to say, no "magic" formulas to call up to affect those problems? Can a man of God take the buffeting, the
pain of relating to the non-Christian and realizing that not everything comes out just great as a result? How much suffering will
or can a man of God take in seeking to bind up the wounds of
innocent victims caught in the cross fire of conflict?

*W*hen Jim Johnson wrote those words as part of a
description of his most famous fictional creation, the Rever-
end Raymond Sebastian, he probably never realized how aptly he was describing himself. One of his own answers to this
what-does-a-man-do dilemma was to write books that "come
to grips with what it costs when a man or woman dares to
reach out to the troubled, hurting, dying masses around us."

With gratitude and acknowledgment to Zondervan Publishing House, for the use of
their files and permission to quote form existing correspondence, and to Rosemary
Johnson, for permission to quote from Jim's letters.

As a writer, Jim always found ground-breaking ways to do that in both fiction and nonfiction. Genre and style were important to him, but beneath his drive to write ran a much deeper and more important desire. He once said that he chose the Sebastian espionage-adventure series with its "heavy plot and espionage milieu because it is popular reading; but the milieu is only the device to bring out my character in his struggle to relate to people outside [the faith]."

I first met Jim Johnson face-to-face when I was a member of a publishers' panel he chaired at the Christian Writer's Conference at Wheaton College. Prior to that, although we had never met, I served as his editor for the first book he published with Zondervan Publishing House, *The Nine to Five Complex* (1972). By then Jim had already earned his reputation as a pioneering Christian novelist, a Christian statesman, and the moving force behind the establishment of the communications program at Wheaton College.

What I didn't know, but soon learned, was that Jim was also the kind of author that editors dream about. He understood an editor's function and role, and he wanted to be edited. Furthermore, he knew how to work with an editor. That became evident from our very first contact.

After I wrote to Jim, introducing myself as his editor and making some general comments about his manuscript, I received a gracious reply, thanking me for my encouragement. In personal conversation he could at times sound abrupt and opinionated, as he often did in his writing style. But in his author-editor, author-publisher working relationships, he was generous of spirit and often self-effacing. In that first letter, he said:

> I appreciate your comments and encouragement. I trust it [the manuscript] will be used to help somebody. . . . That should finish it on my end. I leave the rest up to you and your own good talents.

Unfailingly, in almost every letter I ever received from him, Jim found an opportunity to thank me for something. He always seemed grateful for the smallest things, even those done in the line of duty—such as checking on why something had gone awry in the publication process.

Jim was a "no guts, no glory" writer, and nowhere was that more evident than in the writing of *The Nine to Five Complex,* a book that grew out of Jim's own experience as a "Christian organization man." Possibly this was the most difficult book Jim ever wrote, and a lesser man might well have dumped the project somewhere along the road. But Jim was determined to complete the manuscript, which he saw as a much-needed statement on the state of affairs in the world of Christian organizations, a world he knew intimately. Early in the writing process, he wrote:

> This book is not intended to be either a humorous or tongue-in-cheek caricature of what is certainly a highly sensitive area of Christian endeavor. There is humor, sometimes even a kind of tragic comedy. Sometimes the case histories sound caustic. But that is the nature of the Christian business environment too often. All of it, hopefully, is intended to bring some awareness of the broken fences and the torn-down hedges that, if allowed to remain, can only do irreparable damage to the cause of God.

One of the most telling comments on the need and importance of *The Nine to Five Complex* was made by Peter Kladder, Jr., president of Zondervan Publishing House at the time: "We weren't so sure we should publish this book, because it hits us where we hurt. We have concluded that that is exactly why we ought to publish this book!"

Jim wanted to honor those he called the "forgotten Christians," otherwise known as full-time, paid Christian workers, and in doing so he was bound to step on toes and ruffle feathers with his honest assessments. Yet he never lost his zeal, perspective, or sense of humor: "My friends are fast fleeing the Jonah, and they hope I will jump over the side for Moby Dick to swallow once and for all . . . got any contacts for an excommunicated writer? A PR man? Minister? Garbage disposer?"

Charging full-tilt at issues and topics, whether in fiction or nonfiction, Jim attempted to express the common man's woes and joys, a bit pessimistically and satirically at times, but always with the believer's ultimate hope. That is evident in the closing pages of *The Nine to Five Complex,* when Jim holds out hope for his archetypal "Christian organization man," Alexander Simon:

> The possibility of change, then, lies in the calibre of people whom God must "call" into these organizations. That "call" is primarily for the gifted, trained, experienced, and spiritually mature executive, mainly from the secular business arena, who can successfully man the bilge pumps while trimming the sails at the same time. It calls for men and women who will go into these organizations with their eyes wide open, fully aware of the conditions, the complexes, and the heavy hand of the Patriarch. Such individuals will have to own qualities of forbearance, patience, resolution, and sheer tenacity. It will take love, diplomacy, and wisdom of the first order to work with, through, or even around Alexander Simon to get the Good Ship Grace on course. Mostly it calls for people who will not allow themselves to be stripped of their gifts or their calling but will make their talents and resources felt despite the heavy hand of the authoritarian. These specially anointed people must see their "calling" for what it is, not necessarily a millennial experience or a Mount of Transfiguration, but a commission to put sweat, blood, and even tears into the often gritty mundaneness of business-ministry that is at best a confusing hybrid. And they must see Alexander Simon, not as their enemy or God's who must be rudely bumped out of the way to make room for change, but as a man—and still God's man oddly enough—who is a composite of tremendous needs many of which he is not aware of himself. They must see him in his *potential* then, as God sees him.

About the time *The Nine to Five Complex* came out, he addressed the topic of the book in his *Christian Bookseller* magazine column, "The Last Word." In doing so, he presented a strong statement about his own calling as a writer:

> I would also see in the Scriptures a brutal honest reporting job about the totality of man, even the holiest of them. The Bible reports the saint who at times becomes a louse; it shows the human frailties of people who could one moment praise the Lord and the next chase the smell of mammon. The intent of God in all this, at least in part anyway, was to show that He does not need a fancy Public Relations Department. The journalists of that time showed that the custodians of the Kingdom of God needed to get exposed for their shortsightedness, lack of love, and their bent to pamper the flesh. The prophets, then, were God's editorial writers commissioned to lay their lives on the line to tell it like it is and bring the people to repentance. . . .
>
> At this hour of church history, we need the Christian journalist, or the journalist who is Christian, to fulfill his *total* task. It is not enough to conclude we do God a service by ignoring the seamy side of saintly sin or trying to give it a positive shot of sanctified "right guard." The church needs self-analysis and self-exposure. . . .
>
> But for the record, as a Christian journalist, I cannot violate my total responsibility by simply being an "image maker." I owe it to God, my fellow Christian, even to the non-Christian and certainly to myself.

In 1975 Jim submitted a proposal for another nonfiction work, which he called *What Every Woman Should Know About a Man.* This proposal seemed quite a departure for a writer who was primarily known for his minister-cum-James Bond hero. Yet it was absolutely typical, as was the letter that came with it.

Jim's book proposals were never very polished; they always looked as though they had been dashed off at the last minute, with incomplete thoughts in a flurry of typos (when you worked with Jim you soon learned to read his special brand of shorthand and fill in the gaps for yourself). His letters read as though he were out of breath and running to catch the last train out of town (see example below).

In spite of that, he always managed to nail his basic premise. This manuscript, for which he submitted a prologue and a rough outline, was no exception.

> . . . this prologue gives the tone and the general areas of what I wish to cover . . . the typical marriage of two people, exploring the tension, the myths, the areas where they will need adjustment to each other. . . .
>
> My point in the book is to help the woman to understand her man, that knowing his sexual drive and function and how to complement that is simply not enough to hold the union together. I want to discuss communication in his terms, the lack of it at times, what drives him and what bugs him sometimes in the Christian context. I want to explore for men—who have no real voice as I see it yet in the various books—some of their problems with Christianity [in the] midyears—everybody talks about the poor women who go through a "change of life" and must be understood and cuddled in that change, but women seldom understand what a man goes through in his own "change." I want to explore this from the man's view so the Christian woman will come to an awareness that [he is] vulnerable, often lonely, frustrated, etc.
>
> I want to put this against the backdrop of Christian manhood as I think Jesus had it. His temperaments were not always so constant either in his humanity and the tension of his Deity against that. But in it all I want to share that capacity of the "God man" like Christ to fulfill real manhood with all of its dimensions which the woman needs to know to better understand his struggle to emerge.

It is difficult now, with the proliferation of books on the subject of men and women and marriage, to realize just how unusual it was at that time for a man like Jim to be writing a book like this from a man's perspective for the religious market.

Although modified by faith and divine grace, Jim was a Hemingway, not a Grace Livingston Hill. He was a "man's writer," and to think of him specifically addressing women could have given one pause. It is to his credit as a writer that he was able to move beyond the boundaries of his sex and his background to reach the cutting edge.

> I give you this one prologue now, holding off on the rest of it. If you think it sounds worthy, okay. If you don't that's okay too. In any case, I am going to go through with it, but I wanted you to get a feel for it. Let me know what you think. I need a commitment from a publisher to get it done, as you well know.

This last statement shows another side of Jim, the writer. He was always strongly committed to his ideas and to follow-through once he seriously began a project, but he needed incentive to get started. He was too easily diverted by the varied interests and pursuits in his life (discussed by others in this book). Yet he didn't want the reins held too tightly, as evident in his reply to the contract we offered when we said we liked both the subject matter and the approach.

> I will take the contract, leave date open which I will fill later. No front money until I get far enough down the track to be assured that my manuscript won't misfire. I can't operate under any pressures of specific deadlines or certainly any money that I might have to pay back. But I will be working on it.
>
> In the meantime you mentioned there were problems about my prologue. Too wordy? . . . Okay, that's easy. What about the way I have treated it as a whole? You want it cut down or what? If I know there are emphases that you don't like in it, I know what to steer away from in the manuscript . . . I appreciate your confidence in me for this.

He also included a few comments about a book he had recently published with another house:

> You may have gotten [a copy of] my latest [book] out with [publisher] . . . considering that [the publisher] does next to nothing either in exposing or even shipping books, one of Billy Graham's angels must have been with . . . me on that one.
>
> My nine-to-five complex has moved to 8:30 to 7:30. I still get mail on that book, regardless of sales.

The last comment refers to the fact that despite great reviews, *The Nine to Five Complex* had not sold well. And though Jim was certainly a normal author in the sense that he was concerned about sales and was often frustrated because he could not make enough money from his writing to free him to do other writing, he seemed able to keep his balance. He never took out his frustration on those of us at the publishing end—as many authors did.

Several months later, in response to an invitation to attend the Zondervan author dinner at the Christian Bookseller's Convention in Atlantic City, Jim wrote to say he was working on the manuscript [*What Every Woman Should Know About a Man*] and was thus forgoing conventions and meetings:

> I have really had a rough year in every sense. Totally wiped out with classroom work and Spectrum and ELO and still trying to put across to women what they should know about men. So if I am slow it is not because I have ignored you but because the glands are on strike.

At this point, we reminded him that he had never signed and returned his contract. He responded, saying that he hoped to have it in soon:

I want to be sure I have cleared the hurdle before getting socked into a bind. Medical necessity. Though I am improving in this department, this past year put me back considerably. I was at my lowest productive level to date because of the press of the college, etc. I am still trying to come back off that.

During the years I worked with him, Jim's letters increasingly reflected a man hurtling from one thing to the next, filled with grand ideas but overcommitted, driven, with never enough time.

Late that year, he sent the first six chapters of *What Every Woman Should Know About a Man,* requesting a bit more time to complete the rest of the final draft:

> I started out two years ago to write a "light" book on what a man is all about. But after interviews with sixty couples in this city of faith, I found that this is no light or laughing matter. There are too many Christian couples in this town on the rocks—I mean love has now become diluted with ice. After reviewing all of these some time back and realizing that the wives were charging husbands with "indifference, oversexed, distant, too constantly worried about his own image," etc., I decided I had better get serious with the treatment.
>
> . . . it thusly reads a little heavy. But I felt I had to do it this way in hopes it would be accepted more seriously. I hope I didn't destroy the thing by doing so.
>
> I know I am coming on the tail end of a lot of marriage and women's books, so I am not counting on skyrocketing sales. Maybe you ought to do the thing in paper and save some money. But it's a strange thing: I have held at least 30 Bible study class groups for couples running from [ages] 22 to 42 in the last 18 months and I taught this material in this book. It is amazing, and I was really delighted and yet a bit shook, that what I put across, which is in this book, actually came as a kind of "total deliverance" to a lot of women. Beyond that, the men themselves admitted to me not only that

they were glad I was able to help their wives understand them, but in essence they came to understand themselves much better.

Enough said. I don't mean to rationalize it. I just thought you might like to know what I tried to do here, good or bad, and hope that it can be of some help to people and get your money back.

I have not pushed heavy on the spiritual, but I tried to tie it in where it could be. My emphasis is that the spirituality is the ground for finding understanding and not the total answer in itself. Too much spiritualizing about a man who tosses his socks in the corner instead of the hamper is just too gagging to too many people.

A month later the rest of the manuscript arrived:

Thanks for giving me the time and the extra mile you afforded me. As the Africans say I hope the complete work now will "give your stomach rest." Contrarily, I hope it does not kick up a storm. In any case, thanks for allowing me the attempt. I learned more about myself as a man in doing this book maybe than the woman.

What Every Woman Should Know About a Man came out the following spring, 1977. Shortly thereafter, in one of those unfortunate juxtapositions that are often no one's fault, Zondervan announced another book on a similar subject, *The Husband Book,* by Dean Merrill, which was chosen as the lead title to be promoted at CBA. Many authors would have thrown a fit at this ridiculous timing, but Jim took it in stride with just a dash of sarcasm. When he was asked to speak at the author dinner at CBA that year, he wrote:

I have a CCC [Christian Communications Council] overseas executive meeting at 6:30 that evening and probably wouldn't get out of there in time. If I do get there, I would gladly talk—share a meaningful response to one of my books.

Thanks for inviting me. I see that someone else is the show stopper at CBA—already I am jilted!! . . . but that's publishing.

Anyway, you've done your extra mile for me, and I appreciate it . . . it's been the best exposure I ever had, and I can't ask for more. If it doesn't go, it's not your fault—but if Merrill's beats me out, it is your fault!

I will be up your way next week—if you are all in, I'll stop by with my royal entourage. If you are not, your loss. Hope to see you there; if not you'll see me in CBA walking around with a sandwich board front and back advertising—guess what?

Fortunately, Jim's book did well. It made the National Religious Bestsellers list and was in print for a number of years, in both hardcover and paperback.

In the meantime, Jim had assigned Zondervan the reprint rights for his first four Sebastian books, *Code Name Sebastian, Nine Lives of Alphonse, A Handful of Dominoes,* and *A Piece of the Moon Is Missing.* Originally published in hardcover by Lippincott, these novels had been out for a number of years. Zondervan wanted to do them in mass market paperback, which they did. Zondervan also wanted to publish the next original titles in the series.

Jim also reported that Moody Press was interested in doing a paperback of his novel *The Death of Kings,* originally published 1974 by Doubleday, the large New York trade house.

Doubleday would be delighted, of course, because they aren't sure how to handle Christian fiction in the market either . . . not enough sex to carry the trade, not enough Christian to carry in CBA (or rather just a bit too frank for Christians).

Now I'm going to do all I can to give you a good vehicle in Sebastian to warrant your expenditure. God willing. I hope the Hong Kong one will come across. [Jim planned that the next Sebastian novel, *The Last Train from Canton,* would be set in Hong Kong.] I am not sure how fast the first one can get to you . . . depends again on schedule, on my time and physical limitations. You are kind to allow me this flexibility. If I can get out from under the academic and administrative go-around I am in, I can work better and faster.

I trust we will find this venture successful in every sense and that God Himself would want it to go on, that is [the] Sebastian series. I don't want you to feel any strain in this commitment, however, if along the line it doesn't go, you know we can have a gentleman's agreement about it and drop it. I don't want anyone stuck with me or Sebastian on a long term deal, but your wisdom about a five-title package is good only in that we have a target and some room to prove something.

While his preliminary proposals may have been a bit slapdash, when it came to his writing, Jim wanted to get it just right. I always had the sense that when he sent the final manuscript off, it was with the attitude that he had done what he could as a writer and now he needed the objective input of the editor. However, he did not expect the editor to do his work for him. He was careful to obtain his own permissions and track down anything that needed tracking down.

After editing *The Last Train from Canton*, I sent him ten pages, single-spaced, of questions or comments on details of character, setting, description, and plot. He later told me that he had taken these to his writing class at Wheaton and told them "this is what an editor is supposed to do for a writer."

But, like most writers, Jim was plagued with his own insecurities and days of discouragement:

I must say there are moments when I decide I am going to chuck the novel and find a football hero whose story I can be "truthful" about and at the same time maybe get richer on. Judging by how few people on the average will read my pains-taking effort to entertain while talking meaningfully about life and God, there are times when I sense that I am forever doomed to insignificance. At that moment I am tempted to strive for "significance" which I am told is maybe writing a quick "Hello, God, I am Still Here" kind of book. There is nothing wrong with that, but it may be wrong for me.

I am fully aware on most days, too, that the state of the arts in the Christian culture has not advanced much since Michelangelo refused to wallpaper the basilica and stuck to his hammer and chisel.

Because *The Last Train from Canton* did not sell well, Zondervan was uncertain whether to proceed with any new books in the series and discussed it with Jim. It was difficult for him to watch Sebastian just fade away; as a writer, he wanted to control the demise of his creation.

> As to Sebastian . . . I see the series fading out . . . is the whole idea a dead dog? Maybe spy stories are out? . . . Or maybe . . . well, maybe there isn't any life left?
>
> If so, I then should plan a proper burial for my man Sebastian. But . . . maybe he's not dead yet? Let me know. I am proceeding on other lines of fiction . . . but I don't want to leave Sebastian hanging.

In a strange sort of life-imitates-art, the possible demise of his most famous character seemed to reflect what was happening in Jim's own life. I sensed a weariness, as though his clock was winding down. However, six months after he wrote the above letter, in his typical discouraged-encouraged seesaw fashion, Jim sent the following response when I suggested he move on to the next Sebastian, and perhaps make it the last.

> Thanks for your encouragement to proceed to wrap up Sebastian properly. I think I can do a proper job and leave everyone feeling good. Including marketing/sales. Seems we need to throw in everything that has a mystery/romance in it. I will set it in the South Pacific out of Sydney as planned. I think we will—absolutely—bring Barb Churchill [the heroine of the

series and Sebastian's romantic interest] into this final one out on that 44-foot sailboat.

I will send you the outline soon.

I had also been asking him to do a book for writers, as he seemed, with his experience, to be the natural person to do it.

Thanks too for the suggestion about doing a book for writers. Have had that in the hopper for some time. It could have a very good sale with all the writers I have run across and would-be writers especially.

Unfortunately, we never did either book together. In a combination of time-lag, lapsed commitment from the publisher, and our inability to agree on some contractual arrangements, Jim decided to try to bring the old Sebastian books back into print with another publisher and complete the final book. But we continued our editor-author friendship, with periodic phone calls and letters—Jim's always ending with the promise that he would be coming to Grand Rapids for a visit—for a chat—for a cup of coffee. He never did, but I know he meant to.

Jim Johnson was no plaster saint. He was too real to be plaster. From an editor's perspective, I saw him as a man who wanted his writing to come first, but somehow always had to put it last. He had too many irons in the fire and more ideas than he had time for. And it's only my opinion, but I believe Jim Johnson never wrote the great novel he was truly capable of writing. He just never had the time.

Yet he created a body of literature that has touched countless lives, and he left an unending legacy in the lives of the many talented writers he encouraged. That he had time for.

With gratitude and acknowledgment to Zondervan Publishing House, for the use of their files and permission to quote form existing correspondence, and to Rosemary Johnson, for permission to quote from Jim's letters.

Waiting was not for Jim. . . . He was impulsive and wanted to move ahead, and at times he couldn't see why people dragged their feet.

8

A Genuine Spirit

R. H. (Bob) Hawkins, Sr.

Bob Hawkins, Sr., is the founder and chairman of Harvest House
Publishers, Inc., Oregon. For eight years he was with Tyndale
House Publishers as marketing and sales director. Besides serving
two terms as a director of Evangelical Christian Publishers
Association, he was also ECPA President for three years. He is
widely respected in the book industry because of
his visionary leadership and expertise in Christian publishing
and bookselling. He and his wife, Shirley, live in Eugene.
Their friendship with Rosemary and Jim Johnson, and
their son, Jay, extends over twenty-five years.

*N*either my wife, Shirley, nor our three children
wanted to move to the Midwest. Yet we believed that was
where God wanted us. So we sold our Christian bookstore in
Portland. It was July 1964 when our family left that city for a
new adventure in Illinois. Kenneth Taylor, paraphraser of *The
Living Bible,* had asked me to become part of Tyndale House
Publishers, *Christian Reader,* and some other publications
that were to be started.

Personally, I was concerned about leaving many close
relationships back in the Northwest. Would I meet friends
with the same goals, aspirations, and perspectives that I had
in my bookstore in Portland?

Although I was excited about going into publishing at
Tyndale House, I had reservations. Would I fit in? Could I do
the job I was hired to do? Gradually I felt confident about our
move. I loved the job and the challenge—but I missed my
friends.

In 1965, Shirley and I were invited to a Christian function in Wheaton, Illinois. Christian authors were there. Authors and their ability to write have always fascinated me. That evening I met Jim Johnson, an author and novelist. We talked about books, and I learned of his concern for writing good, sound, solid, wonderful books. Jim also told me about his teaching at the Wheaton College Graduate School where he was the director of the newly established communications division the college had asked him to set up.

I found a real friend in Jim, someone who shared similar philosophies and feelings. We thought alike, and we were both outspoken. Jim was always up-front—no airs, no politicking. His forthrightness and openness provided the soil that nurtured our growing friendship.

At that time, Jim was writing the Sebastian spy mystery series. I'll never forget my reaction when I picked up my first sample from that series. Instantly I knew that this talented writer was far, far ahead of his time. His writings were tight, well structured, and written for the thinking reader with more education than the average layperson. With my Christian book-selling background, I knew the Sebastian books were rather heavy for the Christian market. However, the novels challenged me, and so I encouraged Jim to continue writing the series. After two of his spy mysteries, *Code Name Sebastian* and *Nine Lives of Alfonse,* were published by Lippincott, Jim began to question whether to continue writing spy stories, because sales were average. I encouraged him not to give up, because his material was excellent and far above anything else available in contemporary Christian writing. Jim did complete the Sebastian series, six volumes in all. Four were published by Lippincott

In the midst of his writing novels, I remember talking with Jim about writing a book with appeal to the average Christian reader, one that met the needs of the average, everyday Christian—perhaps dealing with husband and wife relationships. From this conversation came the book *What Every*

Woman Should Know About a Man, published in 1977 by Zondervan. The book sold more than 100,000 copies—much to Jim's surprise! It sold several thousand more copies than the combined sales of his six novels. Jim was elated.

We discussed the reasons this type of book could be so important and sell so well while his Sebastian books, which were much deeper, more intriguing, and more exciting, did not sell as well. One possible reason for the excellent sales of *What Every Woman Should Know About a Man* is that so many Christian books are bought by women. Among evangelicals around 80 percent of book buying is done by women.

Jim had an inquisitive mind and was perceptive about what he believed the Christian public should read and know. If Jim were alive today, I believe he would continue to write novels. When Jim began writing Christian novels they were almost unheard of, whereas today many Christian novels are written and sold in Christian and general bookstores.

Harvest House published five of Jim's books: two novels and three nonfiction titles. In 1981 we published in paperback his 1974 novel *The Death of Kings* (Doubleday) with the title *All the King's Men*, and then in 1985 *The Tender Summer,* a saga of love and courage in Texas in the late 1800s. The nonfiction titles were *How to Enjoy Life and Not Feel Guilty* (1980) followed the same year by a reprint of *Nine to Five Complex* under the title *Profits, Power and Piety*. Then in 1981 we brought out *Scars and Stripes,* a paperback edition of *Before Honor,* published some years earlier by Holman.

Our friendship drew closer. Many times when I was discouraged, pressured, and needing to get away, I'd hop in the car, pick up Jim at his office, and take off for lunch. We'd spend a couple of hours—sometimes seething over mutual problems and frustrations, sometimes sharing Christian publishing concerns. At other times we explored ways to get better distribution not only for his books but for products I was working on as well. Jim constantly encouraged me especially when I became impatient or disillusioned with the Christian book trade. At those times Jim would say, "Don't quit, be patient. Don't give up on Christian books and bookselling or the readers." Jim's words always challenged me.

He cared deeply about others and enjoyed helping people, especially authors. His counsel was vital to the success of many Christian writers. One of his unique skills was the ability to know intuitively what needed to be done to make a manuscript publishable. He also worked far into the night on his students' writing projects. He loved interacting with the graduate students as together they debated ways to communicate clearly what the Christian public really wanted and needed.

Both of us understood wants and needs and tried to separate them, though we believed that was impossible. We knew that "need books" are not often purchased by Christians. People rarely want what they need; they want what they want, which is to have their desires satisfied. Christians are basically selfish and want how-to books that will build them up. That in itself is not all bad, but Jim and I were concerned about publishing and distributing books that would witness and be a help to people in our mixed-up world.

We felt there was a need for books that created a strong desire within people's hearts to serve and to help others have a deeper faith and closer walk with the Lord. That was not easy. On many occasions Jim was depressed as he tried to find a way to create an appetite in his students and others to buy books with deeper significance. What Jim wrestled with is a problem familiar to most of us in the publishing industry. We want readers to read more thought-provoking books.

Jim was greatly loved—maybe not always understood. He was a complicated man because of his brilliance. He was extremely opinionated. Yet, despite his high IQ and multifaceted drives and interests, he was one of the most dedicated men I have ever met. He loved his family dearly. He often talked about his son, Jay, or his wife, Rosemary, who he said put up with him through thick and thin and helped him in so many ways. "Jay is superior in writing," Jim would say. Jim knew that Jay would become an effective speaker and writer. Jay was ordained an Episcopal priest in 1988 and served as interim rector at St. Simon's Episcopal Church in Arlington Heights, Illinois. In the fall of 1991 he began graduate work in doctrinal studies at the University of California at Berkeley, California.

Hardly a day or week goes by without thoughts of our times together, and especially of the lessons of perseverance and persistence that Jim taught me. I often think, *Jim, why didn't you teach me patience?* And then remember—he couldn't do that because he was not patient himself. Jim wanted things done—not tomorrow, but now! I recall the times when Rosemary would say, "Jim, relax and wait patiently for things to happen." Waiting was not for Jim. For him it was now or never. He was impulsive and wanted to move ahead, and at times he couldn't see why people dragged their feet. Jim made the world around him move. I understood Jim well because I, too, fit a similar mold. His impatient quality was one reason why Jim was so special to me.

Speaking at writers' and missions conferences was something Jim enjoyed. He was a stirring speaker, and each time I heard him he had just the right thing to say. Following a talk or message, people surrounded him to ask questions, and he was always willing to advise when asked. He continually gave of himself.

Jim left an enduring legacy to those who knew him well. I miss him very much. He was down-to-earth, an articulate communicator, honest, genuine, hardworking, unselfish, and yes, impatient. He was real! He disliked false piety—he admired spiritual depth.

Our family moved to Oregon some years before Jim died. I traveled a great deal and often called him—at all hours—for advice. Regardless of the hour, Jim willingly discussed book topics with me. Undoubtedly, if Jim were alive today, we would be discussing book ideas and possibly collaborating on some book or books. When I passed through Chicago, we would often meet at the airport. We talked about books—publishing them, distributing them—books, books, books.

That was Jim's life.

These things you need to know.
Know yourself. Be yourself.
Express yourself. Do them and you
will always have something to write.

9
Ruth, Keep Writing.

Ruth Senter

Ruth Senter is the author of six books and is a columnist. She
holds a journalism degree from the Wheaton College Graduate
School. She served as editor of *Partnership* magazine as well as
contributing editor for *Today's Christian Woman* and *Campus
Life*. Ruth has written for many publications, has cohosted the
TV series "Adventures in Learning," and is a frequent speaker.
Ruth's husband is professor of Christian education at Trinity
Evangelical Divinity School. They have two children.

I am young and a novice. Who do I think I am,
walking into this publishing house? I don't even know what a
production editor is, and here I am one! Such are my thoughts
on this bleak September morning as I push open the back
door and walk into the offices of a magazine I've known
about for years. The day is cool, but my hands are sweating
and I'm not sure my legs will carry me down the hall and into
the publisher's office, where I am to meet the managing editor who has hired me and the publisher who is soon to find
out how much I do or do not know about magazine publishing.

I hear voices coming from the lunchroom on the right.
And laughter. They actually laugh here in this imposing red
brick and white pillared structure with its impressive logo out
front. Those who know the logo know that serious journalism
takes place here—birthplace of literature that touches down
on all four corners of the globe. I am some comforted by the
laughter and the smell of coffee coming from the lunchroom.
No graduate school degree. No portfolio of published pieces.
Maybe it won't show. I try to prop up my sagging confidence.

Graduate degrees and portfolios seem the last thing on the mind of the man coming from the lunchroom. He walks directly into my unsure path—coffee steaming in his cup. He stops and holds out his free hand.

"Hello. I'm Jim Johnson." His voice is gentle and gruff at the same time. "You must be the new production editor for the magazine. They said you were starting today. Welcome aboard. It's a great place to be—exciting times for Christian publishing. The literature organization I'm with has it's offices here too." He shakes my hand like he is priming a pump. I feel his energy.

And then I know it will be OK—this my first venture into Christian publishing. His enthusiasm bolsters my sagging spirit. Not only is it going to be OK, it is going to be an adventure—like starting out for a ride in the country on a crisp fall day. You're not sure where it is you're going, but the glories of the day beckon and you mean to follow wherever it is the road takes you. In this one brief moment of meeting, here in the hallway of 330 South Schmale Road, I catch a bit of the fervor and flavor that is to become a part of me—that will shape me and shove me in ways I've never dreamed possible.

It is nearly nine months since that first meeting in the back hallway of South Schmale Road. I am learning magazine publishing. I am the sponge. Taking in. Taking in. Taking in. Learning. Learning. Learning. Over editorial meetings. Over the drawing boards and paste-ups and bluelines. Over galleys and proofs and manuscripts. I learn from the doing and also from association.

"So what are you going to be doing in Christian publishing ten years from now?" Jim asks me today as I munch my carrot and celery sticks in the lunchroom. I keep munching and think hard. No one has ever asked the question before. In fact, I hadn't even asked the question before. I can't think of the answer.

"You need to write, Ruth. I saw the promotional piece you did. Ever thought of graduate work in journalism?"

It was confession time. I had to admit. No, I had not thought of graduate school. And no, I did not have a ten-year plan for my life in Christian publishing. In fact, I was here by default. The job I'd hoped for in radio had not come through. I landed this job more as a fluke than the result of careful planning and creative dreaming.

He is not one to beat around the bush.

"Ruth. You are in publishing by design, not by fluke. I have a challenge for you. I would like you to cover the international literature conference coming up next month." He says it matter-of-factly, as though I've been doing news coverage for international conferences all my life. I sit my coffee mug down with a thud.

"But I've never covered anything before—"

"So . . ."

"I've never even written anything for the magazine yet."

"So . . ."

"I'm not a news reporter—"

"So . . . you're not going to let that stop you, are you? The conference is a worthy news item. It needs to be covered, and you're the person to do it. I've already arranged it with your boss."

When he's decided something, he is not one to give up.

And so I cover the literature conference, ready or not. Jim fills out my registration and marks "press" across the top, arranges my transportation, teaches me to run the tape recorder, briefs me on the schedule—places I need to be, people to see, questions to ask. On the morning the conference begins, I walk into the hotel carrying briefcase, press packet, and tape recorder. So convincing is Jim Johnson that I almost dare to believe I can do it.

And I do it. I listen. Interview. Write. Write. Write. My news story appears in the next issue of the magazine. After its publication, the managing editor calls me to his office. "Ruth. How would you like to do a feature on illiteracy for the next

issue of the magazine?" In the months to come I do less crop-
ping of pictures and more writing of articles. "Keep writing,"
Jim says one morning as I pass him in the hall on my way for
coffee. It is an order, not a request.

"Ruth. Keep writing." How can I forget? It must have
been the way he said it.

Eight years have passed. I am sitting across the desk
from Jim again. It is a different desk in a different building
—this time, offices of the graduate school. My years since the
magazine on South Schmale Road have been filled with having babies, reading Dr. Seuss, playing Candyland, wiping running noses, fixing peanut butter and jelly sandwiches to the
tune of Bozo the circus clown. But always there has been
time for writing—snatches of moments at my typewriter, moments broken up into bit pieces but moments nevertheless.
Always his words come back. "Ruth. Keep writing." And I
have. Today I decide it is time to explore the next step. I have
sought him out.

"Do you suppose it's too late to get started? It's been ten
years since I've been to school."

"Never too late."

"But how many other mothers of two children do you
have enrolling in graduate school?"

"Doesn't matter."

He is intent on the task.

"Now, let's see, I think I will put you in 'Editorial Writing
401.' It's an evening course. Easy on the family. Be a good
one to start with . . ."

"It's not just time in the classroom that worries me, it's
the reading and the writing—and what do I do if the children
get sick or PTA comes on the night of class?—you know,
there are lots of unpredictables when you're a mother."

He doesn't bother to look up. He is not even listening to
my excuses. He scribbles on this yellow-lined pad, shuffles

through the pages of the catalog, and makes an entry on the class schedule work sheet before him.

"Then I think you'd better plan to take two courses next semester, since the class in 'Publishing Problems' isn't offered again till the following spring, and you don't want to let everything go until your final year. By then you will need to be thinking about a creative project—for you, writing your first book."

Writing my first book! Right now it is taking every ounce of courage and energy I can muster just to think about getting through my first course, and he has me writing a book already. I should be panicked.

But as I walk down the stairs and out into the street, with the next three years of my life tightly scheduled, strangely enough, I feel neither exhaustion nor panic. It is a bright fall day again, and I am back on the road. There is a path to be followed. The glories of the day beckon. Sometimes when one is about to take a journey, the ultimate send-off is knowing someone believes in you far more than you believe in yourself. With new courage, I hurry home to fill out my forms for tomorrow's registration.

My fears about being the oldest graduate student on the class roster are not completely unfounded. I don't remember that ten years can make so much difference. And how has my blackwatch wool kilt from Scotland and my forest green sweater suddenly got so behind collegiate fashions? And what do peanut butter sandwiches have to do with the swinging young single from California who has surfed Malibu, participated in Hollywood game shows, and now sits beside me in "Feature Writing 408"? But here we are—bunched together in Buswell Hall, determined to make it through graduate school. Some days I wonder if it can be done.

The day is hot for early spring. I smell the apple blossoms just outside the classroom window and think wistfully that in two more weeks it will be spring break. Three classes done and one to go for the year. There is no air conditioning here in this upper floor of Buswell Hall at Wheaton College, and Jim, the professor, has not shown up even though the bell rang five minutes ago. I sit and leaf through my notes from last class, semiconscious of the buzz of conversation around me. I have taken the last seat on the back row, not because it is the only seat left but more because it is characteristic of my feelings today—last seat, back row.

I do not belong to this younger generation even though we are studying the same things. They are young. Vivacious. Adventuresome. Free to come and go as the urge strikes. Full of experiences and expertise. Sharp minds. Quick learners. Dreamers of dreams. Fulfillers of visions. And besides all that, they can write.

We wait on. I occupy my time with my assignment to be handed in today. It is a feature on a youth organization on the West Coast. I have conducted my interview with great care and meticulously gathered my information. Somehow today, the writing seems dull and listless. Strange that it did not seem so when I wrote it. I wish I'd used more dialogue, less description. But there is nothing I can do about it now.

Finally, Jim walks through the door. For some reason, none of us think of him as Professor Johnson. He is simply Jim. As usual, he comes in a whirlwind. He has rushed from a committee meeting and has another one immediately after class. He will be in his office after eight in the morning if any of us have questions about the critique he is handing back. His critiques are predictable: yellow notebook paper, typed into the margins, some praise, plenty of "wordy. unnecessary. redundant. cliché. vague. what? huh? where did this come from?"

I reach for my returned assignment with the yellow critique paper clipped to the first page. He is the only professor I know who writes full page critiques on every assignment. Reaching for that yellow page is like swallowing mint flavored Pepto Bismol—it is awful and it is good. Awful because I see what I could have done. Good because someone cares enough to type an entire page of critique on my work.

Today his lecture does not dwell on critique. He does not even seem concerned about information to impart. He sits in typical Jim Johnson fashion on the side of the desk, one leg slung carelessly over the edge. He leans forward, into us. We are his group. And he has something to say that has nothing to do with writing yet everything to do with writing. For a moment I forget being in graduate school—"Feature Writing 408." His voice is gentle and gruff at the same time.

"Hear me. Are you listening?"

How could we not be listening? He has the intensity of one about to change the course of the universe. But then, he usually has the intensity of one about to change the course of the universe. I suppose that's why we always sit up and take notice.

"Three things you need to do. *Know* yourself. *Be* yourself. *Express* yourself. Do them, and you will always have something to write."

Simple as that. His lecture is over. He has delivered the goods. He pulls out the desk chair and seats himself off to the side. Someone reaches up for the screen that hangs from the ceiling, turns out the lights, flips on the overhead projector, and we begin our critiques of each other's work.

But I do not hear the critiques. I do not even hear the voices. "Three things. Know myself. Be myself. Express myself." It is as though he has read my mind, my heart, my mood on this warm day in March. And he said it all in three points, six words. Nothing wasted. Nothing lost. I know I will never forget. He has taught me focus, not only in what he said but in how he said it.

By now, I'm approaching the midpoint of my program. The monotony of grad school has seeped inside me. The monotony of life has seeped inside. There seems no existence beyond typewriters and libraries and books and pencils with used up erasers and outlines—miles and miles of endless outlines. I think it will never end—this academic treadmill I'm on. And I am very sure that I shall never again go to bed at a decent hour.

There seems to be no life inside me tonight as I park my car behind the library, walk the half block to Buswell, and laboriously climb the stairs to second floor where the dim blue walls and the dull overhead lights add to my listlessness. How could writing ever have seemed glamorous? Who needs to publish articles anyway? Besides, what do I have to say?

Tonight Jim is on time—there as usual with his limitless energy. But tonight will be hopeless. There is not even the slightest possibility of his enthusiasm rubbing off. I am too far gone.

He plops himself down on the desktop in his usual leg-over-the-side style and proceeds to read a poem. We are caught up into his reading of cosmic significance. (His voice gives it that.) I try to muster concentration to listen.

> I took to church one morning a happy four-year-old boy
> Holding a bright blue string to which was attached his
>   much loved orange balloon with pink stripes . . .
> Certainly a thing of beauty
> And if not forever at least a joy for a very important now.
> When later he met me at the door
> Clutching blue string, orange and pink bobbing behind
>   him,
> He didn't have to tell me something had gone wrong
> "What's the matter?"
> He wouldn't tell me.
> "I bet they loved your balloon . . ."
> Out it came, then—mocking the teacher's voice, "We
>   don't bring balloons to church."
> Then that little four-year-old, his lip a little trembly,
>   asked:
> "Why aren't balloons allowed in church? I thought God
>   would like balloons."

I celebrate balloons, parades and chocolate chip
    cookies
I celebrate sea shells and elephants and lions that roar
I celebrate aromas: bread baking, mincemeat, lemons . . .
I celebrate seeing: bright colors, wheat in a field, tiny
    wild flowers . . .
I celebrate hearing: waves pounding, the rain's rhythm,
    soft voices . . .
I celebrate touching: toes in the sand, a kitten's fur, an-
    other person . . .
I celebrate the sun that shines slab dab in our faces . . .
I celebrate snow falling . . . the wondrous quiet of the
    snow falling . . .
I celebrate the crashing thunder and the brazen
    lightning . . .
And I celebrate the green of the world . . . the life-giving
    green . . . the hope-giving green . . .
I celebrate birth: the wonder . . . the miracle . . . of that
    tiny life already asserting its selfhood.
I celebrate children
    who laugh out loud
    who walk in the mud and dawdle in the puddles
    who put chocolate fingers anywhere
    who like to be tickled
    who scribble in church
    who whisper in loud voices
    who sing in louder voices
    who run . . . and laugh when they fall
    who cry at the top of their lungs
    who squeeze the toothpaste all over the bathroom
    who slurp their soup
    who chew cough drops
    who ask questions
    who give us sticky paste-covered creations
    who want their picture taken
    who don't use their napkins
    who bury their goldfish, sleep with the dog, scream
        at their best friend
    who hug us in a hurry and rush outside without
        their hats

I celebrate children who are so busy living they don't
    have time for our hangups
And I celebrate adults who are as little children
I celebrate the man who breaks up the meaningless rou-
    tines of his life.
The man who stops to reflect, to question, to doubt
       The man who isn't afraid to feel
          The man who refuses to play the game.
I celebrate anger at injustice
I celebrate tears for the mistreated, the hurt, the
    lonely . . .
I celebrate the community that cares . . . the church . . .
I celebrate the church.
I celebrate the times when we in the church made it . . .
    When we answered a cry
    When we held to our warm and well-fed bodies a
        cold and lonely world
I celebrate the times when we let God get through to our
    hiding places
    Through our maze of meetings
       Our pleasant facade
          Deep down to our selfhood
             Deep down to where we really are
         Call it heart, soul, naked self
         It's where we hide
         Deep down away from God
         And away from each other
I celebrate the times when the church is the Church
    When we are Christians
    When we are living, loving, contributing
God's children . . . I celebrate that He calls us His chil-
    dren even when we are in hiding
I celebrate Love . . . the moments when the You is more
    important than the I
I celebrate perfect love . . . the cross . . . the Christ
    loving in spite of . . .
    giving without reward
I celebrate the music within a man that must be heard
I celebrate life . . . that we may live more abundantly . . .

Where did we get the idea that balloons don't belong in
    the church?
Where did we get the idea that God loves gray and sh-h-h
And drab and anything will do?
I think it's blasphemy not to appreciate the joy in God's
    world.
I think it's blasphemy not to bring our joy into His
    church.
For God so loved the world
That He hung there
Loving the unlovable
What beautiful gift cannot be offered unto the Lord?
Whether it's a balloon or a song or some joy that sits
    within you waiting to have the lid taken off.
The Scriptures say there's a time to laugh and a time to
    weep
It's not hard to see the reasons for crying in a world
    where man's hatred for man is so manifest.
But it's also not hard to see the reasons for laughter in a
    world where God's love for man is so manifest.
So celebrate!
Bring your balloons and your butterflies, your bouquets
    of flowers . . .
Bring the torches and hold them high!
Dance your dances, paint your feelings, sing your songs,
    whistle, laugh
Life is a celebration, an affirmation of God's love
Life is distributing more balloons
For God so loved the world . . .
Surely that's a cause for Joy.
Surely we should celebrate!
Good news! That He should love us that much.
Where did we ever get the idea that balloons don't be-
    long in the church?

We sit in silence. No one moves. Finally Jim says, "Do you wish you'd written it? I do."

More silence. Then we return to the world of academics.

I go from this dull blue room out into the night. The embers have been stirred. I unlock the door of my car and notice the harvest moon resting on the tops of the tall pines along the back of the parking lot. "If the moon can hold water, it will rain," my father used to say. I decide the moon cannot hold water so it won't rain tomorrow. I have returned to the world around me. I will always have something to write. I am filled with new hope.

I have dreaded this assignment since the class began. True adventure. I knew it was coming, but today when Jim assigns the article—due in two weeks—it looms like Mt. Everest before me. True adventure. It just doesn't fit my personality. I have lived through very few dramas in real life. The only one I can think of happened one dramatic day when I was six years old. I'd accepted the dare to climb the side of our neighbor's log barn. I'd made it to the roof-line but was not so fortunate coming down. My toe missed the crack and I landed on a jagged piece of broken glass. But even that drama had only a twenty-minute ride to the hospital in my dad's station wagon and four stitches to show for it. How does one create an article out of that?

"Does it have to be our own adventure?" I ask Jim after class. "I'm not the adventurous type. Never been lost in a snowstorm and rescued by a helicopter or stranded on an island or chased by a wild bull."

He is amused, but only for a minute.

"Don't tell me you have nothing to write. Write what's within you. You are experience rich. Mine your experiences."

End of conversation. I know I'd best start mining.

Two weeks later and the article is completed. I have the feeling, though I don't know for sure, that this may be one of my best. When I'd given it some thought, the story was there just waiting to be mined. I had recreated the night six years earlier when at a college reunion, I'd almost choked to death on a chocolate brownie. I described the frightening incident and the painful aftermath, when I'd been so paralyzed by fear of choking again that every meal had become a giant battle-ground with nausea. I told about the struggle and what I'd dis-covered about overcoming fear. The story had written itself.

"How I Conquered a Chocolate Monster" is not only the story Jim decides should be the "model" true adventure piece for classes to come, it ultimately finds its way into a maga-zine, three reprints, and a book. Today, some fifteen years later, I have graduate students tell me they've read my "Choc-olate Monster" story in a magazine writing class.

"Write from within," Jim had said. He assumed all along there was gold within. And he was very convincing, even when I thought there was nothing to mine.

There comes a time in one's journey, when one must go it alone.

I am not ready to go it alone, at least, not quite yet. I am not yet out of graduate school, and I have a book—a "cre-ative project"—to complete before graduation. I am still very much in need of a functioning adviser, not to speak of a men-tor, friend, and encourager. It is not a good time to lose your support base.

But the phone call comes anyhow. Without warning.

"Jim is in intensive care. Critical condition. His heart again. Open heart surgery scheduled for one tomorrow. We are forming an around-the-clock prayer vigil. Would you take three to three-fifteen tomorrow afternoon?"

I agree to pray. It is all I can do. But I think too. I think about Jim and about me and about how I will ever make it on my own in this the final stretch. I have never needed him more. The project sits untouched in my typewriter for three days.

"Ruth. You need to keep writing."

I hear his voice louder than ever.

But I feel like quitting. This book has no ending. It has no life, no punch. I sit and stare at my typewriter and feel the power leaking, like a slow leak in a tire. Six months till graduation but the power is leaking. I have no adviser. He is tied up in tubes in a hospital bed. My heart wrings for him. I plead for his life. For his sake. For my sake. For everybody's sake.

But I must keep writing. For his sake. For my sake. For everybody's sake (he would say).

I plod on, pathetically trying to patch the leak. Draw on the part of him that has rubbed off on me from before. Hope. Determination. Courage. Grit. I am surprised at how much I have received. The flow gradually returns. I sit at my typewriter and write, for days on end, in between the peanut butter sandwiches and the PTA.

We both recover. He from surgery. I from writing the book. He is not around for the process, but he is here for the reward. Pale and thin, he sits on the front row with all the other academic-robed dignitaries as I cross the stage and reach for the navy blue leather that houses reward. The diploma is etched in gold. The degree is mine. In some ways, the degree is his, too.

And today, thirteen years removed from that bright May graduation day, I sit at my word processor. Jim is no longer here. Not at the grad school or the magazine offices on South Schmale Road or in the hospital bed, tied up with tubes. He is not here. He is There in the new Jerusalem with a new heart.

But here on my shelf in front of me is the harvest. Seven books with my name on the cover. He planted the seed. "Some publisher needs this manuscript," he had said after his first reading of my creative project-book. "I will send it in." And he did. Nine months later my "creative project" from grad school was book stock on Christian bookstores across the country. Over the years, that creative-project-turned-book has seen seven reprintings. Today it is in its second edition and awaits translation into Chinese. On its dedication page are these words: "To James L. Johnson, my friend and teacher, who gave me courage to make this offering."

And the courage has lingered these thirteen years, even though courage goes with the ebb and flow. I go with the ebb and flow. Some days I feel like quitting. Some days I think, *I have nothing to say*. Sometimes life loses its spark and words are dull and lifeless and all I can see is my own miserable self. But once upon a time, long ago and far away, someone believed in me. And so I return to my word processor day after day after day. Somehow, I see him up there on the streets of gold, waving a pencil in the air and saying in his gentle-gruff voice, "Ruth. Keep writing."

When God's hand is truly felt and evidenced, the most dramatic outcome often is vulnerability and true sensitivity to the needs of others. These were the characteristics that made Jim such a good friend.

10
A Fellow Struggler

James F. Engel

James F. Engel, Ph.D., is distinguished professor of marketing, research, and strategy in the M.B.A./M.S. program in economic development at Eastern College, St. Davids, Pennsylvania. He also heads up the Institute of Leadership Development. He is the author of numerous books, including the widely quoted *What's Gone Wrong with the Harvest* (coauthored with H. Wilbert Norton, Sr.). In addition, he is senior author of *Consumer Behavior*, a standard textbook used in business schools worldwide. Dr. Engel is vice president of Media Associates International, Inc., and one of the founding directors. He and his wife, Sharon, live in Chester Springs, Pennsylvania.

*M*y experience with Jim Johnson began one beautiful autumn day in 1972 when he picked me up at O'Hare Airport in Chicago. For some reason, Wheaton College invited me, a brash, young Christian from Ohio State University and a newcomer to the evangelical world, to address a banquet celebrating the fourth anniversary of its pioneering graduate program in communications. Little did I know what was in store for me.

After searching for Jim for at least fifteen minutes, I finally saw an impatient guy leaning against the United Airlines counter. Right away I knew that had to be Johnson. He must have come to a similar conclusion about me, because he straightened up and said, "Engel? Let's get moving."

We made that short trip to Wheaton in record time. What a driver—rush off at the lights, slam on the brakes, taking corners like he was in the Indianapolis 500, pushing speed limits to the maximum (or beyond)—all the time talking nonstop about the Wheaton graduate program the Lord had directed him to start four years earlier.

The anecdote aptly describes the vision and temperament of the Jim Johnson I came to know so well—always looking to the future, impatient with status quo, his "on button" permanently stuck on top speed. Few people have made such a great impact on my life and on the lives of the students who came across his path. I can only pray that these few words do justice to such a great friend.

Somehow God seemed to use a similar pattern when he created Jim and me. Maybe that's the reason we became so close in the next sixteen years as we joined hands at Wheaton College, ELO, MAI, and in other endeavors, all of which were positioned at the frontiers of God's work in His kingdom. Some ventures proved highly successful, and others were dismal failures. Over countless lunches we dreamed, commiserated, laughed, and cried.

I have come to see that most true visionaries are a strange mixture of elation and despair. Certainly that was true of Jim. Like one of the figures in Greek mythology, he was always pushing a rock up the hill, constantly struggling to keep it from rolling back and crushing him. Regardless of the struggle, however, he never stopped listening to God and pushing on to greater heights.

Jim was totally captivated by a God-given dream that the mass media, especially the printed page, can and should play a pivotal role making disciples in all nations (Matthew 28:20). Far more than most of his media contemporaries, he grasped that that never would take place without greater vision and professionalism.

To put it mildly, he was less than enchanted with most of the Christian literature that crossed his desk. I can still hear his words—"evangelical pablum," "spiritual junk food," and other less printable epithets. There never was any question how Jim felt about things. For me, that was a refreshing antidote to evangelical blandness.

Yes, Jim pushed the rock up the hill. He never wavered in his prophetic call for writers who could speak to Christians and non-Christians alike with understanding, empathy, and authority. His never-ending quest was to see Christ and His people presented on the printed page without the pious encumbrances that so often depict the Christian as mild, effeminate, ineffectual, and otherworldly.

Jim also was a battle-scarred veteran of the Christian organization arena. He, like others of us, entered this camp after a truly life-changing encounter with the Person of Jesus Christ, carrying along some understandable but naive expectations. He bore deep scars inflicted in the inevitable awakening to the fact that both the people and institutions on this side of the road are not much different from their secular counterparts.

Fortunately, Jim never lost the conviction that Christian organizations can and should be demonstrably different in treatment of their staff and the way they conduct their ministry. He never wavered in elevating the prophetic banner that called for nothing less than the highest standards in those respects. I will never forget the dismay, and even outright grief, that Jim would express when Christian idealism was compromised so quickly in the day-to-day reality of Christian organizational life.

Jim unquestionably held high standards, but that could be a mixed blessing at times. Some of us, myself and Jim included, are temperamentally destined to become driven workaholics. There is an inner voice, often rooted in defective self-esteem, that demands relentless perfectionism. That sense of drivenness can become compounded when we switch our allegiance to Christ. Now we embrace the highest possible cause and find ourselves even more enmeshed unless we are released from the tyranny of workaholism.

Jim was a workaholic right up to the moment God called him home. Nothing any of us could say ever changed that. As he would often say, "I guess I'll stay in the saddle until my grave." It is hard to watch someone you love relentlessly per-

severe in such a destructive path, especially in the context of
the unfortunate demands of his last ministry assignment. But
apparently there was no other way he could satisfy those motivating voices within him.

The outcome is that Jim Johnson was an intriguing mixture of God's hand on his life and call to ministry, unrelenting
inner drives, and uncompromising standards. He could be
exciting and inspirational, on the one hand, because few
could equal his ability to challenge and motivate others to
new heights.

On the other hand, he struggled with the dark clouds of
personal and organizational Christian frailty. That is the "flip-
side" of most true visionaries and motivators, and Jim was no
exception to the rule. In spite of the volatility of ups and
downs, the Lord was solidly in place as the bedrock of Jim's
life. When God's hand is truly felt and evidenced, the most
dramatic outcome often is vulnerability and true sensitivity to
the needs of others. Those were the characteristics that made
Jim such a good friend.

I will never forget the fall of 1980, which was the spiritual Armageddon of my life and ministry. It is revealing to discover how quickly true friends come forward and others fall
away in such times. Jim, as a fellow struggler, was one of the
few who were there at the lowest moments and remained
committed to me when I had the greatest need. He had been
there himself at different times and was drawn to others who
were forced to walk that difficult mile.

"One day when we came to Fiction Writing class, there
was a notice on the door that Jim wouldn't be able to teach that
day. One student threw her books on the floor. 'Doggone it,' she
said, 'I wanted to hear him. He's the best teacher I've ever had!'"

Those words from a former student, Mary Jane Faircloth,
say it all—Jim was a master in the classroom. There were
hundreds of graduate students from all over the world during
the years 1969 to 1982 whose lives were profoundly influ-

enced by his teaching and mentoring. As another student so aptly put it, "I know that I'll *always* remember Jim Johnson. Every student should have at least one professor like Jim Johnson—he was incredible."

His "alumni" overflow with reminiscences and praise. First of all, there is concurrence that he knew what he was talking about. No one ever said that Jim was a boring academic. As Bill Decker points out, it was quite to the contrary:

> He was one of those "authentic" kinds of people, gruff and funny and sensitive. He knew his journalistic stuff, but he didn't have to use ten-dollar words to convey it. We knew he had been out in the African bush, in the editorial offices of big city papers, and with writers from developing countries. He had paid the price of someone who loved his vocation. But he never came across as one who used these terrific experiences to say, "Look how good I am."

Knowledge and experience are only the starting point, however. Few will become great teachers unless there is genuine identification with students accompanied by awareness of their potential and belief in the integrity of their motivation. It is those qualities that most endeared Jim to his students, especially to those who viewed themselves as mavericks who don't quite fit in.

Jim was enough of a rebel himself to be attracted to those who didn't walk to the conventional, evangelical drum. Because he often walked the same mile, he was in a unique position to offer real help. Here is just one story out of many:

> I was going through some heavy soul-searching during my graduate school days, trying to make sense of some deep rooted and unresolved family issues that were refusing to remain ignored. Somehow in the atmosphere of Wheaton I found a trivialization of grief or problems, a kind of disapproval or indictment of the quality of my faith, as if trials correlated with a lack of trust in God. I didn't really know how or

where to channel my unfolding anger and release of emotions, my questions about God, my fears. Ironically, for me at least, the very "Christian" atmosphere pervading Wheaton was also a way of keeping people like me, with our myriad doubts and problems, at bay.

To this student and others, "Jim," to use her words, "was a good friend, a confidant, and human." Although he often did not come forth with specific advice, Jim succeeded in affirming the other person's Christian integrity and encouraging him to grasp the frequently difficult-to-accept Christian principle that true growth only occurs through struggle and perseverance.

As one would expect, Jim's relentless drive for excellence also spilled over into his classroom expectations. Fortunately, most who came to the Graduate School in those days were motivated by a passion for ministry and thrived in that atmosphere. Kelsey Menehan described the atmosphere graphically:

> Jim hated nambie-pambie Christians. I can still picture him marching into our Editorial Writing class (his heart probably pumping much too fast even then) and saying something outrageous designed to get us worked up into a lather. He'd storm right up to people and demand that they tell him what they thought on a particular subject. He'd make us go deeper and deeper, down to the core issue around which we could write a good, hard-hitting editorial. I've never been satisfied with surfacey, sweet articles ever since. Jim helped me to be a better thinker. "That," he said, "was one necessary prerequisite to being a good writer."

Kelsey put her finger on one of Jim Johnson's greatest pet peeves—superficial and trivial Christian writing that ducks controversial issues. Rita (Messino) West was among the first graduates of the "Johnson School of Writing," and vividly recalls how his focus on authentic Christianity and the tough issues shaped her career:

I still cringe when told that someone "received a blessing" from my writing (Jim's translation: nothing there for readers to disagree with). Anger, annoyance, grist for thought, a twinge of conscience. Jim advised us to give our readers anything but a blessing. What he gave us was a heritage of excellence to carry into our careers.

Finally, Jim was a true mentor, committed to taking the time to develop potential to its fullest. I can recall many days when he dragged into the office wearing his gloom-cloud mantle and evidencing genuine fatigue. More often than not, he had spent most of the night pouring over writing assignments.

Although Jim often seemed to go beyond the call of duty, especially when his health was failing, there is no question that that is what it takes to produce top writers. As Mary Jane Faircloth recalls:

> No one whoever took a class of his could ever forget the copious notes he would write to us about each assignment we turned in. Each note was at least half a page, single-spaced, loaded with typing errors and strike-overs, and always on yellow paper. We all marveled that he would write so much for each of us and get them back so quickly—always within 48 hours. The notes contained not only criticisms but also suggestions for improvement.

Jim also helped me become a better writer. I can remember his response when I asked him to read the manuscript of *What's Gone Wrong with the Harvest*. I, too, was the recipient of one of those nearly indecipherable yellow-page notes. His response was that I had seven "land mines" that inevitably would go off and cause me to lose many in my audience unless I softened my approach to some touchy issues. History has provided ample indication that he was dead right, and I'm glad that he said it.

Jim's students will agree with Roberta (Roney) Jezequel who said that "his impact into my life, and into the lives of so many others, goes on living." Unfortunately Jim's classroom days were ended prematurely by an administrative decree that Wheaton faculty must have "advanced" degrees. But he left shoes that *no one else* has been able to fill.

The memory of Jim's death is painfully vivid to this day. I was at home the morning Bob Reekie called with the sad news. I was stunned. Even though most of us who knew him well were fully aware that his driven nature would probably lead to a premature end, I was unprepared. Somehow I had missed some strong signals that he had given to me. Suddenly I realized Jim had a premonition that the end was near, because he scheduled the last of our many lunches together, which I now can see was the occasion for his final words to me.

We reviewed much that we had done together over the past fifteen years and affirmed our friendship and commitment. He wanted assurance from me that all we had built would continue to thrive through Media Associates International, that nothing would interfere in the partnership that he, Bob Reekie, and I had established. He warned me not to be distracted from the all-important priority of motivating and training Christian leaders worldwide.

Later I discovered that Jim had similar lunches with other close friends and associates. Little did we realize that his premonition was to become reality just a few days later.

To this day I miss my friend Jim Johnson. The dedication of my last book, *How to Communicate the Gospel Effectively,* sums up what I have written in this chapter.

To James L. Johnson—my great friend and co-laborer, who influenced an entire generation of leaders in Christian communication. Well done, good and faithful servant—you helped to change the world.

Jim said of his years in the navy, "I made Petty Officer Third in three months. I could have made first but I spent my time at the typewriter writing short stories about the sea." That was in 1944.

In June 1952, Jim and Rosemary Lorts were married. In January 1956 they went to West Africa as missionaries.

AFRICAN
CHALLENGE

Rosemary and Jim

Rosemary and Jim were missionaries with the Sudan Interior Mission from 1956 to 1958 in Lagos, Nigeria.

Jim enjoyed the challenge of being a father to only son Jay Emerson.

"The Africans understood us well. We found them a gentle people."

Jim was editor for the Nigerian Christian magazine called African Challenge. *He wrote, "While I fumbled trying to edit the big monthly magazine, the Nigerians treated us as if we did everything right."*

Earl Roe (left) was assistant editor for African Challenge. *E&
and Jim made a lively editorial team who used every opportunity
to encourage Nigerian writers.*

*Luckson Ejofodomi, a
Nigerian pastor, "was
a born communicator
with a genuine gift for
words." His writing
ability was discovered
and strongly
encouraged by Jim.
Later, Luckson went
on to earn his
doctorate and to serve
on several American
university faculties,
including Harvard.*

After the Johnsons left Nigeria in 1958, Jim never lost sight of his goal to provide opportunities for training Christian nationals.

Jim's first novel, Code Name Sebastian, *was soon followed by another in the series called* The Nine Lives of Alfonse.

Jim had great respect for the broadcast media. He saw print and radio as complementary and strategic for evangelism.

God gave Jim the ability to speak winsomely and powerfully.

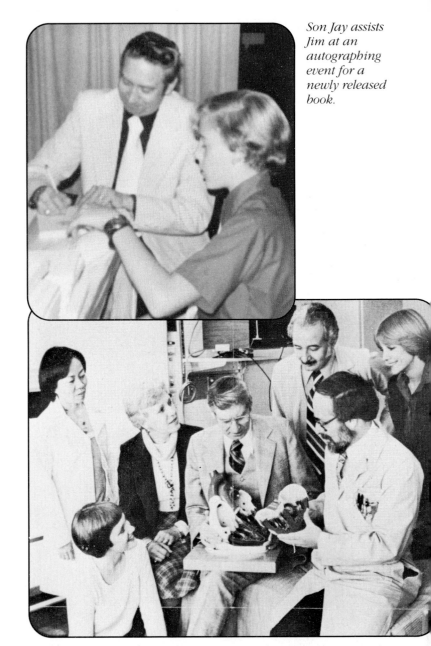

Son Jay assists Jim at an autographing event for a newly released book.

In 1979, Jim Johnson wrote Coming Back. *He said, "I wrote* Coming Back *to pay tribute to the medical and nonmedical people who gave me reason to keep going. The book was good therapy for me." Here, he is with the cardiac specialists at Central DuPage Hospital, Winfield, Illinois, in celebration of his successful open-heart surgery performed in 1978.*

Rosemary and Jim celebrated their thirty-fifth wedding anniversary less than three weeks before he died on June 25, 1987.

Jim's life was spared long enough to see his son, Jay, graduate from college, but he did not witness his son's graduation from seminary. Jay and his mother share a moment of pride following his ordination as an Episcopal priest.

One of Jim's loves was the sea. When he was writing his last novel, Trackless Seas, *published in 1987, he went to Australia to complete research for the novel. He was accompanied by his son.*

Relaxing was never easy for Jim. But when he did find time he enjoyed the breaks away from the pressures of work and his typewriter.

"Our task is to work with national writers ... they alone can reach their own people with the right words."

Long before Christian missiologists became enamored with cross-cultural concepts, Jim was teaching and advocating audience-targeted communication in missionary outreach.

11
Visionary Strategist

H. Wilbert Norton, Sr.

H. Wilbert Norton, Sr., is director of the doctor of missiology
program and professor of Christian missions at Reformed
Theological Seminary in Jackson, Mississippi. For six years he
was executive director of CAMEO and prior to that professor and
director of the missions program at the Wheaton College Graduate
School. Dr. Norton was founding principal of Jos ECWA
Theological Seminary of Nigeria (SIM, International). He was on
the board of Evangelical Literature Overseas (ELO) for many years.
He and his wife, Colene, live in Clinton, Mississippi. They were
missionaries in the Belgian Congo (now Zaire) during the forties.

*J*im Johnson handed me an old black and white
photograph taken years before.

The Brownie-type picture showed Jim as a boy, stepping
out of a second-story window with a shovel in his hand. The
blown snow reached that far up the house—piled so high
that the door was smothered, and Jim had to jump out a second-story window to clear away the snow.

Johnson treasured his boyhood home in the Upper Peninsula, Michigan. He thrived in that rugged Copper Country
where, as often as not, the unconventional was conventional.
Two-story snowdrifts were to be conquered!

The Copper Country peninsula juts almost halfway across
Lake Superior, exposing land and people to the vicious winter storms from the north, east, and west. Dollar Bay had no
protection against the snows of Keneewah County that drifted
to the gables of the modest houses in Dollar Bay.

The climate of his boyhood days helped develop a determination that Johnson demonstrated as an adult—an ir-
repressible urge to do the impossible.

After God transformed Johnson spiritually, he began to gain a vision of what God could do through mass media. Soon after marriage, he and his wife, Rosemary, went to Nigeria with Sudan Interior Mission (now SIM, International), where Jim served as editor of the *African Challenge* magazine (1956-58). His tenure as editor of *Challenge* magazine cut new paths in missionary thinking about literature.

In Nigeria, Johnson quickly saw what literature could do for the church's worldwide missionary outreach. Jim's vision was fivefold:

1. Foster cooperation between mission agencies and the church in literature publication and media development
2. Implement audience research to shape and package messages for spreading the gospel
3. Develop indigenous national leadership and self-supporting production of publications and media
4. Encourage formal and informal education of reporters, writers, editors, producers, and directors involved with Christian publications and media
5. Organize literature and communication fellowships to encourage coordination, education, and cooperation

In trying to fulfill that vision, Jim became an instructor/teacher of publishing for missionaries and their agencies. He became a curriculum designer for both formal and nonformal education. He became a developer of missionary communicators and a researcher-strategist in cross-cultural literature. As a result, he motivated high school and college students, mission executives, national church leaders, college administrators, and business leaders to take literature seriously.

Long before Christian missiologists became enamored with cross-cultural concepts, Jim was teaching and advocating audience-targeted communication in missionary outreach.

Johnson insisted that each person must hear, read, and learn of Christ in a culturally relevant medium.

A Moody Bible Institute alumnus, Johnson returned in 1958 from his first missionary experience in Nigeria to advance his writing skills at the University of Michigan. Professionally prepared Christian journalists were not common in world missions during the sixties.

When Jim became executive director of ELO in 1963 he assumed a mountainous task. Ten years earlier, a group of Christian leaders founded Evangelical Literature Overseas (ELO) to reinforce the missionary enterprise with literature. At that time evangelical Christian literature was often a helter-skelter publishing effort to provide tracts for evangelism, biographical anecdotes, translations of evangelical "classics," and a rare culturally relevant creative piece by a national author.

Many sincerely motivated missionaries and their agencies were obsessed by the idea that the chief resource of a literature program was the printing press. Jim felt a need to abolish the "printing press syndrome." After one of his trips to Africa, he reported a conversation with a missionary whose press was printing a Christian classic for *everyone to read.*

"What is the literacy rate here?" asked Jim.

"I don't know," replied the missionary. "I hadn't thought of that!"

Soon after joining ELO, Johnson targeted Christian high school students. He initiated an innovative program called TYPE (Training Youth for Printed Evangelism). TYPE was a two-year course. More than four hundred students registered for career counseling, guidance tests, and a seventeen-lesson correspondence course covering all phases of missionary writing and production.

He planned, developed, wrote, and graded lessons for students who enrolled in TYPE. Six scholarships were granted annually to qualified students through the program. Most of the students were preparing for literature programs in the Two-Thirds World.

Meanwhile, Johnson's research showed that hundreds of literature opportunities existed on the mission fields. Mission agencies were appealing regularly for personnel. To recruit qualified literature missionaries on Christian college campuses, Johnson initiated EPIC (Evangelical Publications in College). By working with the college administrators and faculties, courses of study in missionary journalism and publishing were introduced. As a result, EPIC graduates began publishing ministries overseas after completing summer internship programs organized by EPIC.

Regional workshops were started by Johnson to complement the annual conferences begun by his predecessor, Hal Street, the first executive director of ELO.

The first regional workshop was in November 1965, at the headquarters of the Christian Literature Crusade in Ft. Washington, Pennsylvania. High on the agenda were literature problems related to evangelizing 68 million francophone Africans. Workshop sessions also focused on Christian literature for East Europeans, Muslims, and Latin Americans; reading materials for new literates; evangelistic advertising in local newspapers; distribution methods; principles of writing and editing; developing successful correspondence courses; and management for literature production. Clinics provided evaluation of missionary literature and ways and means to improve the printed page.

From the beginning Johnson promoted indigenous principles in literature production. At the 1965 regional conference he had Nancy Deischer, a missionary with the Overseas Missionary Fellowship, report on her working relationship with Indonesian national leadership. She asserted categorically, "I don't work over nationals, with nationals, but under nationals." Deisher continued, "I am responsible to an Indonesian in the publishing house. Though he runs things considerably different from an American missionary, I have learned to fit into what he expects of me, as would any other employee."

Johnson planned and promoted international literature conferences and seminars. For example in 1966 he spearheaded major international conferences in Nairobi, Kenya; Bouake, Ivory Coast; São Paulo, Brazil; and Paris, France.

Within five years as executive director of ELO, Johnson opened ELO offices on every continent. Each office was responsible for regional workshops on all facets of literature development, research, and marketing. The offices helped mission agencies set priorities and develop and coordinate literature production.

He was instrumental in bringing about literature fellowships to foster cooperation and sharing of ideas. Examples are: Centre de Publications Evangéliques, established in Ivory Coast, to serve nine French-speaking African nations; Evangelical Literature Fellowship of Nigeria to serve thirteen West African mission agencies; Asia Evangelical Literature Fellowship (AELF) in Singapore to serve Asian interests.

Soon after the AELF was formed with five Asians and one missionary, Johnson brought national leadership into focus in Christian literature production. For the first time Asians discussed Christian literature work and their leadership role face-to-face as Asians.

One outcome was clear recognition of the urgent need to develop a core of national authors to produce books pertinent to local issues facing the churches. Many missionaries admitted they did not recognize the value of training Asians for literature ministries. Their confession was a significant breakthrough.

Johnson also pushed for instructional literature for new Christians. Correspondence courses, Bible studies, books on doctrine and Christian lifestyle are "absolutely essential to hold these new converts in the Body," Johnson said.

The nonformal efforts to train and develop nationals and missionaries for literature programs was significant but inadequate for the challenge in Johnson's view. To meet the awesome demand for quality literature, Johnson believed that a more structured, formal, academic program of research and communication theory was needed at the graduate level to properly equip modern literature workers.

His concern was shared by other print, radio, and audio specialists. Johnson invited nine Christian media agencies to meet in Chicago to discuss closer professional and working relationships among print, radio, audio, and film media personnel. The nine organized an informal professional group called Christian Communications Council (CCC).

Significantly, CCC formulated a proposal petitioning Wheaton College to establish a graduate program in communications. Johnson had a primary role in preparing and presenting the CCC proposal. The action of the CCC was the catalyst leading to the beginning of the Graduate School of Communications at Wheaton College.

The chief goal of the program proposed by the CCC was to establish a graduate program in communications research and theory for furloughing missionaries, national church leaders, and overseas missionary candidates.

Jim Johnson established a date to meet with Wheaton College to present and advocate the CCC proposal. The Wheaton College Administration and Board approved the graduate communications program proposed by the CCC, with the understanding that the college would not be responsible for funding it.

The Graduate School of Communications began in the fall of 1968. At that time, I was directing the Wheaton College Graduate School missions program, which had been started three years earlier. During the sixties I had also been on the ELO board. My belief was and still is that world missions and communications are the heart of world evangelization and church planting.

Johnson was named acting coordinator of the communications program in the Wheaton College Graduate School. Because Wheaton College did not fund the program, Johnson raised monies for the fledgling program. Foundation funds and other gifts kept the program viable for the first three years. Then, in 1971, the college included the graduate communications program in its academic budget.

Undergraduate speech/communications faculty taught courses in the new program. Adjunct faculty with academic qualifications and/or professional expertise supplemented. The audiovisual department provided hands-on instruction. Print communications students gained hands-on internship experience at *Christian Life* magazine in Carol Stream.

Merrill C. Tenney, dean of the Wheaton Graduate School, wanted to ensure that Wheaton's academic standards were implemented in the new graduate communications program. Therefore, in the third year, an evaluation of the program was carried out by the college under the direction of Mel Lorentzen, professor of English. At a graduate school spring dinner, James Engel, professor of marketing at Ohio State University, was the speaker. His message emphasized the application of marketing principles to world evangelization. He electrified the communicators in the audience.

Following that dinner, Jim Engel accepted an invitation to teach a graduate level course each semester during the next academic year. It soon became clear to me and to the graduate faculty that Engel belonged at the graduate school. Engel was invited to become a full-time faculty member and communications researcher. He accepted.

Johnson discovered a new asset. Jim Engel not only had a rich academic track record but provided a superbly qualified Ph.D. for the program and thus fulfilled the academic criteria stressed by Dr. Tenney. The two Jims began a new era in mission communications with a strong emphasis on effective research, long a goal of Johnson's. Engel applied his expertise in marketing to audience and communications research. As a result, research studies were to become part of missions communications and Christian literature programs.

Johnson had set the stage to make research indispensable. His vision, determination, and indefatigable drive to establish literature as a viable medium of world evangelization led mission agencies into a new appreciation of cross-cultural communication and audience research. To improve world evangelization effectiveness, the graduate missions and communications programs were coordinated. That was a giant step forward, linking the *what* (the gospel) to the *how* (the means of communicating the what) in the post-World War II era of missions.

Johnson and Engel complemented one another's gifts and expertise. Cooperation, coordination, and team spirit within the graduate communications department led to amazing enrollment growth and a steady stream of graduates. A 1983 Wheaton College printout lists more than three hundred alumni from the communications program, filling significant positions in media for world evangelism.

Regrettably, some college and graduate school faculty discounted Johnson's abilities because he did not hold a Ph.D. In fact, he did not have a master's degree. Those in academia were incapable of observing and appreciating the quality of his research, brilliant teaching, and powerful writing. They failed to appreciate the editorial gifts he demonstrated in *Spectrum,* the Graduate School of Communications organ so widely received throughout the world.

How ironic that neither Wheaton College nor any institution of Christian higher learning regarded him worthy of recognition by awarding him with an honorary doctorate.

Few fully comprehended how much Johnson was achieving through ELO and how great a physical toll it was taking on him. The endless pursuit of finding money for ELO's program was demanding and exhausting.

ELO's ministry had been accelerating annually, stretching the funds to the limit. Mission agency funding was minimal. Chasing sponsors was a constant endeavor. Foundations carried the heavy end of the financial load for operating and salary expenses. By 1973 a stressed Jim raised the question of

ELO's viability with the board of ELO. Nothing resulted. No serious action was taken by the board to insure viability.

The ELO program demanded more staff and an infusion of money or a merger with an agency that could provide personnel and the funds. Mergers were considered and in some cases explored with media agencies such as David C. Cook Foundation, Moody Literature Mission, and Scripture Press Ministries. Another possibility was to have a commission carry on ELO's ministry under joint sponsorship of the Evangelical Foreign Mission Association/Interdenominational Foreign Mission Association. Nothing came of merger feelers put out by Johnson.

Because of the unresolved financial problem and no imaginative ELO board action, Johnson reluctantly resigned from ELO in May, 1974.

Jim's love for ELO's ministry caused him to submit himself for "reinstatement as ELO executive director" in October 1974. He would continue as instructor and coordinator of journalism at the Wheaton Graduate School and put in at least twenty-five hours a week at the ELO office. He also expected to travel and attend meetings for ELO. Jim felt keenly that this was what God would have him do and asked for prayer.

Four years later, in March 1978, Jim underwent massive heart surgery. Following a long but miraculous recovery he tried to pick up the reins once more. That was a stressful time for Jim Johnson. In the end, he left his teaching post at the Wheaton Graduate School and the leadership of ELO. In 1982, he accepted a senior position at World Relief where he served Christ tirelessly until his death in June 1987.

Jim Johnson was an Elijah type. He faced impossible situations but trusted his God and worked his calling faithfully—until the fire came down!

As I reflect now on Jim's vision, drive, and commitment to the Lord Jesus Christ, I see a blend of unique gifts.

1. He was a print *strategist,* laying out the ways and means to effectively develop literature to win men and women to Christ and to nurture the churches.
2. He was a *teacher,* leading students to understand and apply communication principles in sharing the good news.
3. He was an *inspirer* of those capable of sharing their money for worthy literature projects. That inspiration developed confidence and financial partnership. He never thought of himself as a fund-raiser.
4. He was a *visionary* who longed to see all the media coordinated in the witness to Christ. He struggled to overcome divisiveness and isolationism that characterized so much of evangelical media ministries. He so wanted all media to come together with mutual respect and concern. That dream never happened during his lifetime.

*He simply served people quietly,
without show, behind a typewriter
or telephone . . . and with an
unquenchable zest for the
here-and-now joy for life.*

12
New Beginnings

Marlene Minor

Marlene Minor is deputy associate executive director of the resource development division of World Relief in Carol Stream, Illinois. She began her journalism career as a reporter and editor for Gannett Newspapers. After completing her course work at the Wheaton Graduate School she went to work as a writer at World Relief. She writes for various organizations and publications. She and her husband, Tom, live in Yorkville, Illinois.

I knew Jim Johnson when he was at the end of things.

His last year at Wheaton College Graduate School.

His last job as an executive at World Relief.

His last book, *Trackless Seas.*

It took me five years to recognize how the end of things for Jim signaled a whole new beginning in my own life.

I first met Jim at the Wheaton Graduate School in 1981. I had been assigned as Jim's graduate assistant. Our days—in my mind—were blurs of graded papers, overhead transparencies, and a line of students outside his office. Young people always wanting his advice, a piece of his time, or just a chance to share a lighthearted moment during the pressure of postgraduate studies.

But for Jim and me, it was different. Maybe I was the reason Jim and I did not have his typical student-teacher relationship. Nineteen eighty-one was not a good year for me. Having worked for five years as a journalist for Gannett Newspapers, I was used to variety and excitement every day. Meeting politicians. Interviewing celebrities. Spending evenings with longtime friends. Bringing home regular paychecks.

In graduate school I went to the same classes on Monday, Wednesday, and Friday. Never met celebrities. I lived in a one-room, cinder-block walled, efficiency apartment. I spent ten dollars a week on food at Aldi's Supermarket. And my nights were spent listening to my ninety-two-year-old neighbor's hacking cough through the walls. My paychecks as a graduate assistant didn't begin to pay the bills of living in a Chicagoland suburb and paying tuition fees.

During "the worst year of my life," I ignored Jim and everyone else I could at the graduate school. I didn't want to get to know anyone else at the school—especially Jim. From what I saw of Jim, I knew he would be just the person to unmask my feelings. I watched him do it with other students. Whenever they seemed to have a problem, they went to Jim. But I was going to be different. I was not going to break down and have him solve my problems. I would limit our interactions to brief, hallway encounters in front of his office.

Jim would hand me scribbled notes he wanted put on transparencies. I'd say, "You want these typed out so someone can read them?"

"No—just as they are," he'd snap back.

Despite my distancing techniques, Jim did his best to show he cared about me. For example, one day he called me into his office and asked, "Are you doing OK here?"

I looked around his office. A jumble of books and papers. *He should worry about how this office looks—not me,* I thought. Outwardly, I just answered, "Yes, I'm fine. Got any work for today?"

"Why don't you take any of my classes?" he probed further.

"Well, I'm trying to get through here in a year. And I've got to get these basic requirements out of the way," I replied. "Besides, I'm not good at fiction." (I had heard he was the master of novels.)

Grabbing my assignments off his desk, I headed out the door. I wanted to avoid any revelation of my feelings to anyone in 1981. I thought I had made a mistake coming to graduate school. But I didn't want anyone else to know.

I had come to Wheaton with high hopes. I wanted to get a degree from a Christian school so that later in life I could train other Christians how to do good work in the secular environment of journalism. To break down and tell Jim why I was miserable would admit a weakness. I hated my choice of Wheaton Graduate School. Saying so out loud might diminish what I thought was my "calling" to prepare to teach others.

I didn't want to admit that truth to myself, let alone to a bespectacled, gray-haired professor who held the secrets and disappointments of half the student body. I knew that, based on his experience as a journalist, he could worm information and emotions from me. So my best course of action was to stay clear of Jim Johnson and all his concern for people.

Continuing to protect myself, I rushed all my exchanges with Jim. It was easy to slip past him, because he always seemed to have more than an average workload. Jim was a Type A personality—never stopping, except for people, and never saying no to a new challenge.

Jim would come rushing into the office of the Wheaton Graduate School with a stack of papers for his students. Attached to each student's assignment was at least one page of comments. His hand-scrawled critiques explained how to develop the character better. How the setting could be improved. I secretly hoped students I taught in the future would not expect that much from me. No wonder he always looked tired!

Later, I would discover more about his fatigue. Why he would poke his fingers up under the edges of his glasses to rub his eyes. Why he would sag in his chair. It was not easy to find out why he always looked so tired until you had known him for a while, because Jim was not a person who liked to talk about himself. But I would learn a couple of years later that he almost died during heart surgery—then promptly wrote a book about it.

Jim founded organizations and schools and spent countless all-nighters writing or critiquing the writing of others. And, of course, there were those people he mentored and counseled. For those who felt lost, alone, or depressed, he always made time. All at 105 percent. The long hours and personal sacrifices took a toll on Jim's body. He refused to do any of them halfway. Seaman. Husband. Father. Journalist. Pastor. Missionary. Author. Educator. Christian leader. And friend.

In 1981 I didn't realize how much I could learn from Jim. But in 1982, I caught a first glimpse of what God had in store for me by meeting Jim Johnson—at the end of his life.

If Jim had been a story assignment, I would have researched every aspect of his life. But he was never going to be a page one story, so when it came time for me to leave school in May 1982, I left, never expecting to see Jim again.

I returned to newspaper work. Once I got my job I didn't like the town, the relationship I was in, or the newspaper where I worked. Determined that 1982 should not follow the pattern of 1981, I quickly returned to Wheaton—just to find temporary work and a more positive direction for my life. Imagine my surprise when I landed a "temp" job answering phones at a nonprofit corporation called World Relief and saw Jim strolling through the office.

He looked at me and waved, "Hey, when are you going back to school?"

For the next several days, we exchanged hellos and his when-are-you-going-back-to-school greeting. Neither of us expected to be working together for the next five years. But by the end of the summer, Jim became the head of fund-raising and communications for World Relief, and I was hired as a writer to work in his department.

Having known Jim for a year, even superficially, I knew he cared about people. I remembered the long meetings he had with students in his office. The painstaking critiques of their writing. The arm around a shoulder of a student who looked "down." But Jim just didn't strike me as the type to rally folks to help the starving masses. He seemed so full of joy with others that spending long days to save lives seemed almost too serious a task for the fun-to-be-around Jim Johnson. At least that's what I thought.

I guess I expected a Christian leader in his position to come into the office looking somber at the task before us. After all, forty thousand people were starving to death every day. Our work was life and death, but Jim's focus was different. He wanted us to recognize the severity of the world's suffering people, yet he often injected humor into his work to help us all keep a balance in the midst of the grim realities we were exposed to each day. Because Jim cared about the "living" as much as he did the dying, everyone in the office seemed to beam in his presence. We all liked him. He made everyone feel good after they saw him, no matter how hard the task was before them.

Jim was especially good for morale when funds were low. Even the accountant bean-counters had to laugh when Jim put on an army helmet and marched into budget meetings saying, "OK, let's have the bad news."

Jim's approach to his job of fund-raising (an over 5 million dollar annual responsibility for him) was different from other fund-raisers in the 1980s: he would not publicly "cry and beg" for the people he wanted to help. He simply served those people quietly, without show, behind a typewriter or telephone—and with an unquenchable zest for the here-and-now joy for life. During the height of the Africa famine of the mid-1980s, I would walk past Jim's office and hear him talking on the phone to denominational leaders about the needs of churches in Africa trying to keep their congregations alive.

"Brother, I know you've got things going on at headquarters. I just wanted you to know that whatever you can do to help will mean so much in saving lives," Jim would say.

And as soon as he finished the phone calls, he would turn to his typewriter. Bang out a letter to raise funds. Write a column to stir people's awareness of the problems. Compose a letter to a major donor thanking him for his generous support.

"Whenever I think of Jim, I remember his enthusiasm," recalls Doug Shaw, former church relations director at World Relief. "We would be sitting in a meeting trying to come up with an idea for raising money to help people, and someone would throw out an idea. Jim would always grab hold of an idea and make the best out of it. I can still see him sticking a finger in the air and saying, 'Yeah, that's a good idea.' He was an encourager," Shaw remembers.

After Jim died, Shaw was asked to describe Jim in one word. His choice: joy. Joy seemed such a strange characteristic for someone to display in an occupation so filled with death and despair. But Jim's approach was a reflection of his faith. He never saw masses of starving people. He never saw whole generations wiped out by war, starvation, and greed. He simply saw one person at a time. One creation of God to be saved, touched, cared for.

"Five thousand hungry people. A Judean hillside. Frantic, almost desperate disciples," Jim once wrote.

> How would they feed that crowd? The image in my mind of hundreds of thousands of starving people across the world. People God made me accountable for in some measure at World Relief. For a half hour before I opened the scheduled Scripture reading that day, I confessed, 'Lord, I am not big enough, rich enough, powerful enough to meet the needs of the masses . . .'
>
> So now I faced John 6 . . . then, one line suddenly popped out at me. The Lord had asked His disciples about where they could get food . . . all to test them.

And Peter said, "There is a lad here." Jesus blessed that boy's meager offering of five loaves and two fish and fed that multitude. So, it's not stature that counts . . . or how much money. It's our humble sense of 'smallness' to Him that makes the difference. To become broken bread and poured out wine for the masses. That He will bless and multiply.

Jim wrote those words only a couple of months before he died, but it showed me that God could take someone like Jim—tired and in poor health—to heal the lives of other broken people.

Jim's compassion for people was obvious. But that commitment went deeper. He lived every day to see people as Jesus did—one person at a time. He avoided the trap of seeing the masses. Taking only the "big picture" view makes us vulnerable to paralysis, he would say, allowing us to wallow in inactivity because the problems are too great, the numbers too massive, the resources too small. Instead, Jim took on responsibility, caring for one person at a time, as did his Master.

As I had time to spend with Jim, I learned more about how God had molded him to see the value of each individual created by the Lord. I learned that Jim and I both came from rural areas in the Midwest. Had started working young. Had broken in our "writing" teeth in the rough and tumble newspaper world. In long conversations, I learned our similarities ended there.

His recognition of a need to help the world's poor and suffering stemmed from his own childhood experiences of hunger and poverty. Once, Jim, after much coaxing, shared this story:

> I remember the late years of the Great Depression in my hometown very well, even yet. I remember it for the lack of food, fuel, and the inability to understand why.

More particularly, I remember one cold February afternoon, waiting out back of the grocery store for the butcher to come out and share some of the leftover meat scraps with us.

There were three of us boys waiting, hopping from one foot to the other to keep warm. Finally, the butcher came out holding a pan of fatty, wilted meat chunks in his right hand—the kind that probably wouldn't even make the grinder for dog food today.

He smiled, gave us a cheerful, "Hello, boys!" and leaned down to hold the pan out toward us. I moved forward quickly. But the other two boys were bigger and pushier. They managed to grab most of the meat from the pan before I could get to it. I stood there in total dejection looking down at the skimpy, miserable pieces of gristle. My mother would hardly be able to feed six of us on that. The butcher turned to go back inside, then paused and looked down at me and my woefully meager ration.

"Hey, boys," he called out to the other two already hurrying home with their bounty. They stopped. "Come back here." Slowly, reluctantly, they came back, clutching their meat scraps closer inside their coats.

The butcher jumped down off the loading dock, reached out, and took two pieces of the meat from each boy and gave them to me.

"Never forget what is just, boys," he said to them. "What is fair and right."

I went home that cold, February day with a new faith in the humanity and justice of man. That butcher kept half the town alive on his meat scraps which allowed us to see the day when we could make it on our own.

Jim had been on the other side of suffering, so he knew what it felt like to hurt. He never lost compassion for those in pain—whether physical, spiritual, or emotional. His ministry of caring was extended to one person at a time—every person he came in touch with knew that he cared deeply. Jim's pastoral personality enabled him to serve people from all walks of life—from the mailroom to the boardroom, from the student to the professional.

Jim's constancy to act as Christ did gave him a quality that was valued wherever he worked. It was especially essential to Jerry Ballard, former executive director of World Relief.

"After Jim died we felt a real void—a void of conscience," Ballard said. "If we said anything, or our actions implied inconsistency with Scripture, policy, or previous commitment, Jim would call us on it."

"Jim was also consistent when it came to action and people," Ballard claims. "Jim never liked theoretical problems. He wanted to know, 'What can we do right now?'" Jim's right now was a commitment to people. Whether it was individuals who were starving overseas, or those with whom he worked day in and day out.

"I would get very frustrated with Jim because of his management style and how he handled his staff," Ballard says. "It took my daughter to explain it to me. She said, 'Daddy, don't you see, Jim's not running a division. He's a teacher.' He managed people that way. He taught them. Let them learn from their own mistakes. He fought for his staff even when I thought someone wasn't going to cut it. He saw potential in people."

According to Ballard, Jim's commitment to helping suffering people intensified after his painful struggle coming back from open-heart surgery. Jim's experiences as a missionary, pastor, and writer enabled him to feel hurts of distressed people.

Jim was one of those people that you really wanted around during the difficult times. I recall one particularly bad year: 1983. Donations were down and costs had to be cut so World Relief could give help to as many people as possible. Jim had to cut his already small staff in half in just a few days. I watched those experiences age Jim.

He knew the cutbacks had to be made, and yet he agonized over every decision. Even when the numbers made sense, he could not dismiss the emotions each person would feel when he lost his job. Dark circles grew darker under his eyes. His shoulders sagged more than usual. His smile did not come as quickly in the morning.

Day after day, each layoff "victim" was called into Jim's office for the bad news. A name was called, and an employee walked into his office knowing that bad news was coming. Afterward, I expected to see people angry, crying, storming through the halls. Instead, most emerged patting Jim on the back, saying, "It will be OK. Don't worry about it." I don't know what he said to those people, but I'm sure that he continued to display his genuine interest for them in the same way he would a starving farmer in Africa. One person at a time. That unique gift of tapping into people's own sense of need—to be ministered to and to have the opportunity to minister—never eluded Jim. The gift was undeniably genuine.

He often hid his feelings for the world when you talked to him. But when he sat down before a typewriter he could not hide the pain he felt for others who did not know Jesus. Once, when funds were tight, Jim wrote a letter to a denominational partner who had just sent in a gift for $240,000. Jim "hesitated to even ask for more, but I did ask for his prayers." Three weeks later, that leader sent a check for $100,000 with this note, "I'm glad you asked."

Jim's sense of knowing when to ask, knowing when to push, knowing when to kick someone into action, transformed my own life.

I remember Jim's encouragement especially on the days when it was difficult for me to write. I faltered when I thought that no matter what we wrote poor people were going to die. Jim would tell me after I'd written something, "Let God use those words to do what needs to be done. Those aren't your words, Shorty [referring to my five-foot-two-inch frame]."

Other days, when I looked tired or sick, Jim would tell me, "Go home. This place will be here tomorrow."

Those simple words of wisdom marked just the day-to-day exchanges I shared with Jim. But one event in particular would forever change the direction of my life. It began with my own self-denial. I had made clear to Jim from the beginning of my stay at World Relief that I would serve the best I could but that my plan was to return to newspapers. I was not going to be saddled working with Christians. I wanted to be where I could witness to nonbelievers. What better place than newspapers?

"Before you dismiss how God might be able to use you here, why don't you take a look at how the rest of the world lives?" he prodded.

"Well, I wouldn't mind going overseas, if that's what you mean," I replied, eager for a chance to see exotic tourist spots.

I'll admit I was uncomfortable by the gleam in Jim's eye when I agreed to the plan. Weeks later my immediate supervisor told me I had three days to get ready for an overseas trip. I should have been suspicious when Jim organized a bon voyage party that came complete with snake-bite kits for me.

As Jim probably could have predicted, God used that Central America trip to forever change the way I saw the rest of the world. I went with an unspoken sense that people were poor because they did not work hard enough. After three weeks in the jungle, I learned that people worked very hard just to stay alive. I remember in particular the man who asked me if I wanted to see his fields, which he had just planted. I said, "Sure." Two hours of trudging through the dense jungle —and we came to an opening where he had planted enough corn and other vegetables in hopes of keeping his family alive. He had cleared the fields by chopping down trees, hacking through thick vines, and burning jungle underbrush. Daily, he would walk four hours to till the soil, pull weeds from the fields, and labor in the steamy sun.

When I returned, I knew that my work was important. We could make a difference in the lives of people—just by giving one farmer tools to make his work go a little faster. I told all my goriest snake and sickness stories to everyone else. But I told Jim my more serious thoughts about how God could really change the lives of these people—if we helped. Jim encouraged me to put my feelings about people I met on paper as soon as possible.

"Never forget their names," he reminded me.

That advice would help me to see people as God (and Jim) did—one person at a time.

Having been around the world a couple of times now and in dozens of countries, I have to admit I don't always remember their names. But I can recall every face of each person I have met. I remember their specific stories of suffering—because Jim helped me to see them.

I remember

- the nine-year-old boy in India who begged me to buy sex or drugs from him so he could eat
- the seventeen-year-old African mother who walked for three days to get help for her dying child
- the fifty-eight-year-old missionary in India who traveled halfway across the world to teach Indians how to read and later changed his ministry when he learned they could not read if they starved to death

Jim helped me to see these people just as Jesus saw the lad with the five loaves and two fishes. Not because Jim preached to me. Or taught me great management principles. But because he lived as Christ did. With a heart for each person, recognizing that each individual was lovingly created by God.

Jim's last years at World Relief were frustrating for him. He confided to one staff member that he was not doing what he wanted to do. He felt he was not really touching lives at the scene of the action—and when he couldn't, he felt he was failing. Had I known that before he died, I would have told him that he was preparing a whole generation of us to "touch" lives around the world. Writers. Missionaries. Managers. And just friends.

How very fortunate I was to know Jim when he was at the end of things. I learned from Jim and his years of experience. His ability to cross cultural and economic lines, to relate to people where they were. His sensitivity to individuals. His dedication to mirror the steps of the Master.

Jim changed the direction of my life by forcing me to see people as Jesus did. To recognize the value of each individual. To dedicate myself to that vision. Jim's end signaled a new beginning for me.

He saw interaction of print and the broadcast media as complementary and strategic for greater evangelism penetration and effect.

13

A Prophetic Voice

Ben Armstrong

Ben Armstrong was, for twenty-three years, executive director
of National Religious Broadcasters (NRB), an agency serving
more than 1,450 member radio and television stations and
program producers. Before coming to NRB he was director of
radio at Trans World Radio. Dr. Armstrong is the author
of *The Electric Church*, published by Thomas Nelson
in 1979. Presently he and his wife, Ruth, live in Madison,
New Jersey, where he serves as a consultant.

*I*n 1987, as executive director of National Religious
Broadcasters (NRB), I wrote to Jim Johnson's widow, Rosemary, expressing condolences. In my letter I said, "More
should be told about the great contribution that Jim made to
the world. No one will know how much James Johnson as an
author meant to literature, education, missions, and the needs
of the poor and the destitute. For me, Jim will always be remembered as a bright light in a sea of blurred images."

Jim was indeed an unusual person. He was a prophet in
the field of media, way ahead of his time. His understanding
of media use for communications provided insight not discussed in National Religious Broadcasters circles twenty-five
years ago. Yet today, that idea is well accepted in NRB meetings.

Even after his death almost five years ago the implications of Jim's early thinking are intriguing not only writers but
broadcasters. Multimedia and multicultural operations as en-
visioned by Johnson are being introduced in such countries
as Brazil, Nigeria, the Republic of China, and the Philippines,
where broadcasters are working together with those of other

media. The New Life 2000 program sponsored by Campus
Crusade for Christ is another illustration of the kind of multimedia cooperation advocated by Jim. By cooperating with local churches and missionary radio stations, the project seeks
to present the message of Christ to every person by the year
2000 through a combined strategy of training and evangelism
featuring the *Jesus* film.

I first met Jim at the North American Broadcast Section
of the World Association of Christian Communication (NABS-
WACC) Conference, Ft. Lauderdale, Florida, at the Galt
Ocean Mile Hotel. Being a guest at a beach resort, Jim wore a
T-shirt. Throughout the conference, he kept a low profile.

I knew Jim was an author of sixteen books and a professor of journalism at Wheaton College Graduate School in Illinois. But for me, the Wheaton College connection and his
reputation as an author held much less interest than what I
personally observed of him. He knew how to communicate a
message nonverbally as well as by words. His style was informal and low-key. Jim was a keen listener, and when we
talked, what I said really mattered to him. He responded with
empathy. I also observed that although he was an authority in
journalism and print, he remained a fellow learner. I liked
him, and my admiration increased over the years.

Religious communication, explained Jim in his NABS-
WACC talk in Ft. Lauderdale, must be multimedia as opposed
to one medium, such as print. At the time, I was engaged in
religious communications in Christian radio. As director of
Trans World Radio for eight years, I thought the most effective way to reach the world was by radio. I was convinced
that the radio medium was nondebatable. Jim proposed a
new concept—not one medium but multimedia. To me, his
concept was revolutionary.

At first I was taken aback. Then intrigued. Here is what
he developed for the two hundred delegates at the NABS-
WACC conference.

Jim Johnson's concept of media strategy included diversified means to winning the lost for Christ, not merely one medium such as radio or print. He foresaw a time when a specific country would be reached by interaction of many media—not only print or radio, which were predominant then.

What was necessary, he insisted, was a combination approach interrelating radio, TV, film, satellite TV, drama, direct satellite service (DSS), storytelling, and cable TV. In those days, cable was new and reached only 21 percent of the homes in the United States.

Many Christian authors were not as conversant in the broadcast field as they were in the print medium. But Jim Johnson was. He believed the broadcast media could prepare the soil for reception of the gospel. His approach to gospel broadcasting was not confrontational but always cooperative. He saw interaction of print and the broadcast media as complementary and strategic for greater evangelism penetration and effect.

Jim Johnson was a futurist. With his wise perception, he saw what might be possible and was already burgeoning. Related to his vision were two key concepts: multimedia and multicultural. Not many even thought about them then. But thirty years ago, most were shortsighted. Now many agree that Jim was right. Subsequent events have proved Jim Johnson to have been a prophetic voice. Somehow, he had it in focus all along.

I was moved when Jim talked about his new book *Coming Back* (1979, Springhouse Publishing) at the Evangelical Press Association Convention in Nashville, Tennessee, in 1979. Jim spoke poignantly of his recent bout with death following a massive heart attack in 1978, of the power of prayer and its miracle-working efficacy, and of his subsequent spiritual journey and recovery.

Jim suffered and gave public credit to the Lord who had sustained him through the heart crisis and brought him back to life through a miracle healing. Jim never peddled his *Coming Back* experience for audience response or personal financial gain. In the field of religious broadcasting there are some well-publicized cases of evangelists using miraculous healings for the purpose of fund-raising and audience-building, but Jim was not like that. You knew he had gone through the "valley of the shadow," but it was a personal experience never to be exploited.

After his close-to-death encounter, Jim was not the same person. There was something intangibly deep and at the same time expansive about him. He measured time not like an elderly person referring to imminent and impending death but simply with greater urgency in getting various groups together on projects. Jim said, "This is working smart. We can be more efficient this way." His ecumenism meant the practice of it and not talking about it.

One evening in 1984 Jim and I left an Amsterdam hotel to take a walk. In earnest conversation both of us forgot our location. By midnight, we had no idea of our whereabouts. We were lost! Only after walking miles and asking many strangers for directions, did we find our hotel. Jim opened his heart and mind that night in a most candid manner and shared something of his great vision and concern for Third World peoples.

Our miles of conversation revealed a man who was a concerned-for-others kind of person. In fact, he had a certain vulnerability, not because he was unsure of himself but on the contrary because he was inwardly secure. Jim Johnson had inner serenity and so could examine a question frankly and honestly.

Jim communicated with all segments of the church—denominational, nondenominational, fundamentalist, or charismatic. He was a New Testament ecumenicist. His personal ministry and writing reached evangelical circles and the church-at-large.

Jim had a missionary heart and mind. There was no place on earth that he wouldn't go to be of help to communicators and persons in need. You cannot think of Jim without thinking globally. Christianity, to Jim, involved the penetration of Christ into every culture. Asia, Africa, South America, Europe were not continents. They were challenges and opportunities.

Many times I telephoned Jim; sometimes it was for a friendly chat, more often for advice. He was the kind of person you could trust with delicate questions.

One time, I asked Jim if I should invite Malcolm Muggeridge of England to the National Religious Broadcasters' convention in Washington, D.C. I explained that several of the NRB people had serious questions about Muggeridge's Christian faith. Could he, as a former Communist and an editor of *Punch,* be an evangelical to be trusted? If he were accepted by the secular world as a top critic, could he also be one of us? Jim said, "I've read his writings and consider Malcolm a genuine convert to Christianity. I'd recommend you invite him, Ben." Somewhat reluctantly I took Jim's advice and invited Malcolm to NRB.

Though the invitation seemed risky, I remembered Jim's advice and pursued the invitation. Muggeridge accepted and gave three days of lectures establishing beyond question his conversion and biblical convictions. In the midst of a questioning press and secular Washington, D.C., audience, he clearly showed himself to be a humble follower of Christ.

Surprisingly, the day after the convention, the *Washington Post* featured three full pages about NRB. It was a positive report ending with a question. Malcolm Muggeridge was great, but how did he get invited to an NRB convention? The question was rhetorical, and to my knowledge, the *Post* reporter's question was never answered. It would have been a simple answer: Jim Johnson, because of his major role in the invitation. During the press conference following the NRB convention I spoke of my reluctance and Jim's enthusiasm about Muggeridge's lectures. In fact, I said: "How wrong I was! How right Jim was!"

Though he was a master of the printed page, Jim did not see his job as a one-genre effort. He was more concerned about the ultimate objective than the specific form being used. Others talked methods. Jim discussed strategy. Johnson developed a communications strategy characterized by two words: *multimedia* and *multicultural.* Jim did not see print as the sole medium. Instead, Jim believed that film, broadcasting, TV, cable, print, storytelling, and the spoken word were all viable means to convey the message of Christ.

"By every means possible," Jim said. What made Jim's words prophetic was that at that time hundreds of media people and agencies were "doing their own thing." Why not? They were called of God to a particular media ministry. Jim did not question their call but urged multimedia strategy even though there were problems of jealousy and differences of theology, style, and economic realities.

Balancing the concept of multimedia was Jim's equal stress on the multicultural. He was a pioneer in multicultural emphasis. In Jim's view it was unthinkable for anyone to approach gospel evangelism without taking into consideration the culture of the persons to whom the message was directed. Culture had to be the second great factor in world evangelism. Jim exclaimed, "Without an understanding of culture you cease to be a missionary."

When Jim Johnson applied the word *cultural* to media strategy he used the word *multicultural.* To me that was an appropriate application. I should mention that when Jim first introduced multicultural ideas in Holland in 1984 there was great conflict. Jim was at that time chairman of the World Evangelical Fellowship Communications Commission (WEFCC). The multicultural emphasis raised a question. Was multicultural an idea for American missionaries who had worked abroad for years, or did it belong to those who were truly nationals, who were born in the area? Jim handled well the protests of both missionaries and nationals. At times the discussion grew acrimonious. Indigenous nationals brought their arguments, and American missionaries told their story.

It was a classic debate moderated admirably by Jim. His experiences in Africa, Asia, and on other continents gave him insights and sensitivity to cultures, languages, and mores.

Though the debate did not resolve the issue, there was no ambivalence on the meaning of multicultural for Jim Johnson. The word *multicultural* had experiential meaning for Jim. It was not abstract or theoretical.

Multicultural meant working among and with peoples of all races, nationalities, economic status, religions, and ideologies. Jim enjoyed working with men and women of the Third World. While chairman of the WEFCC, Jim traveled extensively worldwide guiding and consulting with Christians involved in media. One of his constant concerns was for media strategies that brought Christians together in their gospel outreach.

"Christians cannot afford the luxury of going it alone," said Jim Johnson. "The stakes of world evangelization are too high because it involves the eternal destiny of never dying souls. Nothing less than interactive and coordinated global action of all media with multicultural awareness and sensitivity, can meet the challenge of world evangelization."

Despite the anger—or maybe because of it— we both began to realize that our woundedness could mean only one thing. We really did love each other.

14
Following the Gleam

Jay E. Johnson

Jay Emerson Johnson was ordained an Episcopal priest
in 1988 and at the time of the writing of this tribute
to his father was interim rector at St. Simon's Episcopal
Church in Arlington Heights, Illinois. In the fall of
1991 he began graduate work in doctoral studies at the
University of California at Berkeley, California.

*T*he call came at 3:30 A.M.

Out of the sleepy fog I heard the phone-voice say, simply, "Your father has had some kind of attack. The paramedics are here. You'd better come down."

I was in my last year of seminary, in a school just barely into the Wisconsin snowbelt. But the call came in mid-June. As the adrenaline pumped me awake, I found myself throwing the strangest things into my overnight bag: a bottle of cologne, beach clothes, Dad's favorite Neil Diamond tape for the car, and, for some reason, a bottle of wine.

As I sped through the rolling farmland and acres of forest surrounding the seminary, a predawn mist covered the edges of the country road, occasionally swirling past my windshield; it made that trip seem even more surreal than my reason for being there. The headlights kept shining off the eyes of small animals as they scurried back into the cover of darkness. "They're a symbol," I said to myself through the tears. "As long as I don't hit one of them, he's still alive."

Deep down in that place in all of us where denial simply does not work, I knew intuitively that he was, in fact, not alive. I could not help but think that this whole affair—the early morning call, the frantic packing, the surrealism—all of it would make a great story. That's what Dad would think. That's how I knew him—not as a writer but a storyteller.

He had been working on a commemorative book for his hometown located in the Upper Peninsula (U.P.) of Michigan. There, my Aunt Bea owned a bottomless coffee pot. I remember sitting around her kitchen table all those many summers of my childhood listening to the Johnson clan tell stories through the endless flow of caffeine and sweets. Neighbors, people who had lived in the same house in that tiny lumber-mill town for generations, wandered in and out from first light to hours past my bedtime, offering their pieces to the storytelling quilt.

August was always the year's highlight for Dad. It meant our annual escape—not just from the rigors of job stress but the torture of hay fever. With his first sneeze came the expected cry, "Time for the U.P.!" The late summer ritual would continue. Toward the end of that eight-hour car trip Dad would say, as if on cue, "There, you smell that? We're almost there." Just then the roadside sign would soon appear: "Welcome to Copper Country. You are now breathing the cleanest, freshest air in the world."

I suspect the air quality of that place, surrounded as it was by field after field of goldenrod, was not the attraction, although, by some miracle of grace, he never seemed to sneeze up there. Every August was a pilgrimage, a journey back to those roots he loved so dearly. There he was not the big city pastor, the burgeoning author, nor even the graduate school star. He was simply Jimmy, son of a Swedish potato farmer, as he used to say frequently. He was just one among a host of storytellers.

For me, it was another opportunity to laugh until I ached, listening to the slapstick stories of a family trying to grow up during the Depression. Children huddled in the kitchen around the wood-burning stove, the only source of heat during those severe winters. The same stove behind which some unsuspecting child would go flying after being whacked across the mouth for talking back, or "giving lip," as Dad put it. Grandma's Swedish accent lilting through the now hilarious story of electric, blue balls of light bouncing between brass bedposts during a thunderstorm because someone neglected to ground the newly purchased lightning rod.

I remember those drives back to Chicago, my speech patterns temporarily transformed by spending so much time with cousins, aunts, and uncles who seemed to end every sentence with "eh?" For eight hours I would recite every U.P. story I could remember, making sure I got the facts right; making sure the punch line was not delivered too early; making sure the gestures punctuated the proper sentences; making sure I would not forget. I wanted to remember, not just the stories, but the time I had spent with my father; time I knew would soon, once again, be in short supply.

From my earliest years all I can remember with much clarity is simply that Dad did not work from nine to five. I had some vague awareness of Dad as a teacher, sometimes a preacher, and always a writer. In both of my childhood homes he consistently retreated to his basement study—the "hole," he used to call it—and disappear into some mysterious, unknown project. Sunday afternoons would occasionally bring a round of football in the backyard, or "shooting some hoops," even the rare trip to the local park district for sledding during the winter. But usually, Sunday afternoons (not to mention the rest of the week) brought the perpetual clacking and rhythmic "ding" of his IBM. That's how I knew he was home. The constant rattle of fingers flying across a keyboard filled the house. I worried about my sanity when I began hearing the familiar tapping even when he was not at home, so ingrained was that clatter in my consciousness.

Contrary to popular wisdom, being an only child is not glamorous, especially when one's father is a writer. There was more to it than relishing the wide-eyed Christmas envy from those kids who came from big families and who were amazed that I received more than two gifts. There was no sibling banter around the dinner table. I could make no brother-ly confidences about what current peculiarity our parents were perpetrating. Dinner with the family meant just the three of us. And more often than not, Dad's mind was elsewhere—to some exotic locale by his tireless imagination. Other hus-bands and fathers may have been locked behind the morning paper; my Dad disappeared behind a "writer's stare."

Everyday life among the local kids was not always easy either. Dad did not have a job like the other dads. A carpenter lived next door for a while. My best friends, three houses down, had an electrician and phone company employee for a father. Two houses on the other side there was even a dad who did something as exciting as drive a bus for the Harlem Globe Trotters.

"What does your dad do?"

"He's a writer."

"Oh," was the polite, usually perplexed reaction. Even I was not sure what that really meant.

As talented as my father may have been at what he did, it made little difference to an eight year old who watched oth-er dads rewire their houses, build clubhouses from scratch, and talk about short-wave radio sets; all of which were com-pletely beyond my father's comprehension. Sometime shortly before turning ten I remember waking up in the middle of the night and hearing voices in the living room. I discovered the electrician (from three houses down) tinkering with an elec-trical socket that had apparently short-circuited and might have been a fire hazard. I should have realized how fortunate we were to have someone nearby who made "house calls." Instead, I wondered why *my* dad couldn't do that.

When Dad's teaching began influencing countless young-er writers, he decided to wear yet another hat: Literary Agent. He began his own agency, "Johnson/Johnson" he called it, complete with stationery and business cards. This was my big chance, I thought, and wasted no time in telling the other kids that my dad had not only just started his own company, but he was the president.

"Oh yeah," they said, "what kind of company?"

"A literary agency," I said, as if he had just been made CEO of a multinational corporation.

"Oh," they said, with the same polite perplexity.

But I was determined. When I was old enough to take an excursion beyond our little neighborhood, I convinced my friends to go with me to the college and sit in on one of Dad's classes. We hopped on our bikes, found old Buswell Hall on Wheaton's campus, and hiked to the third floor conference room. Sitting in the back we fidgeted like restless racehorses in a stable for all of ten minutes before we had had enough.

My friends, needless to say, were not impressed. But even though I cannot remember a single word of that class or even the topic, I was certainly impressed. I was amazed to see him in action. He had the class laughing. The energy was high. Whatever it was he was saying, he said it with a kind of conviction, power, and authority I had not witnessed at home. I had this image of living with a double agent. At home he was just my dad, but at the office he was on a mission—mysterious, urgent, and rarely talked about.

I was too young to read the first of his Sebastian novels when they were first published but was intrigued enough by the fact that they were spy books. When my parents finally bought that CB radio I had been pestering them about, I did not have to ponder long what my "handle" would be.

"Breaker 1-9," I said into the mike with a newfound technical confidence.

"Go ahead, breaker, this is Road Runner. Who've I got there?"

"Ah, yeah—uh, 10-4, Road Runner, you got Sebastian here."

"Come again, breaker."

"Sebastian."

"Who?"

Time for another handle.

There were times when Dad's mysterious vocation paid off. Attending the Christian Booksellers Association convention one year I shared some of his spotlight at an autograph party. I felt important then, checking the stacked inventory of his latest novel, methodically handing him the next one on the pile to sign for, what seemed to me, a gushing fan.

I may not have listened very intently during those occasions when he preached at the local Free Church. But I knew he spoke with power. I realized you could hear a pin drop when he preached. And I enjoyed any spillover notoriety that came my way. I do remember the story he often used about being mistaken for a United States diplomat in a South American country that had the congregation in stitches. An old favorite of his was the one about dropping through a hole in the platform while preaching on the mission field in Nigeria, completely disappearing from view. I sat spellbound one morning listening to his wild tale about running from a tornado on Interstate 80.

But his Charlie Chaplin-like antics were never the punch line in his sermons; he left that for the gospel. For him, I realized, the gospel was the best story he could ever tell. He seemed to realize better than most that his story was worth telling only because his had been woven into God's story— the story of grace. An ordinary son of a potato farmer, he used to begin, wandering through a junior college and the rough-and-tumble life of the navy, with no real direction or purpose, was somehow called by God. And that, he used to say, is grace.

Something of the importance and consuming passion of his work did make its mark on me even early on. At the ripe old age of ten I began a local neighborhood newspaper conveniently reproduced at Dad's office. I started writing the first chapter of a science fiction book, which I was convinced would be the first novel published by an eleven year old. (I never finished it.) His missionary zeal began to percolate in me as well, and I produced several issues of the "Lyon Street Good News," which were reproductions of Sunday school stories for my neighborhood friends. I even daydreamed about teaching and tried setting up a classroom in our basement for the local kids. (They were not exactly excited, however, by the prospect of more school during the summer.)

But then, of course, adolescence hit. And with it all those teenage issues that make life something akin to wandering through a hormonal fog. Dad was at the zenith of his career then. He was teaching full time at the Wheaton College Graduate School: grinding out books; leading writers workshops across the country; globe-trotting not only to research his next novel, but to inspire indigenous writers and publishing houses in whichever corner of the world he happened to be. The great communicator, author, and teacher was making his mark on everyone he met—except his son.

Mercifully, I suppose, that adolescent haze kept me from seeing his absence very clearly. By then, especially as an only child, I had grown accustomed to figuring out life's various complexities without a great deal of input from Mom and Dad. There never had been an older brother or sister around to observe and from whom to make certain discoveries. Going it on my own just seemed to come naturally. Besides, few teenagers take very seriously what parents say anyway.

Then, in 1978, my junior year in high school, Dad was in the hospital. The heart problems that had begun to appear some eight or nine years earlier could no longer be ignored. It was my first *real* crisis. Not just because the bypass surgery had not gone well, or that the surgeon was not being optimistic, but because I realized, for the first time, that I had no idea how I felt about my father. We had never expressed our feelings to each other about anything. The compassion and concern expressed by so many of his friends and colleagues simply did not resonate with what was happening inside of me. I realized, with a shock, that the man for whom so many people were praying, and even expressing anticipatory grief, was a man I did not know.

He did, in fact, survive that ordeal. And, typically, he wrote a book about it. I should have considered it rather strange that I had to read that book before knowing what that experience really meant to him. But that was the established pattern: a busy father and a distant teenager, both peeking around the corners of life at each other, too scared to speak. So I was rather amazed to read in that book that for him, life would be different. We must take time to smell the roses, he wrote. Life is too short—and on and on.

Indeed, life was too short from my perspective. I was unwilling to try and rebuild any of those bridges that may have been burned. I was unwilling to challenge him with the evidence that life had not changed for him, that he was working just as hard, pushing his energy to the limits just as often. Besides, that might mean expressing how I really felt about him, and that was too threatening. I was getting ready for college, after all, and connecting with my father was the last thing on my mind. Even going to the school where he taught, I would still be moving out. I had my own life to live.

Holidays were a different story. While working up to some kind of nostalgic anticipation of going home (even though it was just across town), the reality never seemed to match the fantasy. Dad spent most of his time, as usual, in the "hole." Dinners were customarily quiet, the conversation disjointed. Shortly before returning to school one Christmas break, Dad suddenly appeared from the bowels of his study waving some computer forms in my face while I tried to watch a movie.

"Here, fill this out," he said. No introduction, just the usual flurry of sentence fragments his students had learned to cherish as a charming eccentricity.

"What is it?"

"Career aptitude test."

"But—"

"Just read each question and decide between a, b, or c. I can run it through the scorer this week." And just as quickly, he vanished back down the stairs. He knew I had been struggling with postcollege plans. Career counseling had become a large part of what he did with his graduate students. Many of them had found just the right niche for their writing skills through his various connections in the publishing world.

But at that moment the movie's outcome far outweighed any concern for career aptitude. So I took my time pondering a question or two during the commercials. Not long after, he reemerged asking for the answer sheet. I told him I hadn't finished, and he grabbed the test out of my hands saying I wasn't supposed to take so much time. "It's supposed to reflect your first, gut reaction," he said.

"Oh yeah? Well, I'm not one of your students, Dad!" I exploded, shocking even myself with the outburst. I jumped up from the sofa and stormed to my room. But not without a final jab over the shoulder. "What next—are you going to grade me on being your son?"

That Christmas holiday ground to a halt, and I went back to school earlier than expected. It was the closest we had come to really fighting. And I would have preferred more fights. At least then we might have started expressing some feelings.

Later that same year he decided to retire from teaching. I was out of the dorms by then and in my own off-campus apartment. Mom called early that fall to tell me that the Wheaton Graduate School planned a surprise award banquet for Dad. Would I like to go with her? Not really, I wanted to say. And somehow she knew I would have problems with listening to a string of testimonials. But I reluctantly agreed and a few weeks later met her at the Billy Graham Center, the new home for Wheaton's graduate programs.

The second floor was packed with people, all gathered to honor the man who had founded the communications department. I tried to be pleasant during dinner making small talk with people I barely knew. And then it began. Student after student, teacher after teacher, including the president of Wheaton College, offered their praise for this man who was more than a teacher, a "guiding light"; more than a career counselor, a "spiritual mentor." Each speaker was like another sharp blow to the head as I listened to what this man had been to everyone else but apparently had not had the time to be for me.

I left early. I was seething as I drove back to my apartment, where I began pacing the floor in a rage that actually frightened me. For someone who, four years earlier, had no idea how he felt about his father, I was getting in touch with such a load of resentment that I was about to burst. When I answered the knock at the door only to discover my grinning parents I told them, simply, to sit down and listen. Never before had I unleashed that kind of anger—on anyone.

"Do you have any idea what it's like," I shouted, "to listen to people describe your own father and realize you don't even know him? Do you know what it's like to wonder why your father can be so many things to so many people and not even one of those things to his own son? If teaching and writing means ignoring the people you love, you can be sure I'll have nothing to do with that glorious career!"

And on I went. Both of them just sat there while I ranted and raved. And to their credit, they listened. As I look back on it now, he took a lot from me that night. When finally I had expelled as much anger as I thought possible, I looked at Dad and realized I had just wounded him as much as I felt wounded by him. For both of us, that night was the cork-popper. Despite the anger—or maybe because of it—we both began to realize that our woundedness could mean only one thing. We really did love each other.

But how do a father and son reconnect? How does one start mapping such uncharted territory as feelings? Talking? Risking being vulnerable? Nether one of us could figure out where to begin or even to acknowledge that we wanted to begin whatever it was that was missing. I tried working with a school counselor for a while, but that seemed like a dead end.

Appropriately enough, the new connection began through church. I had left my childhood spiritual tradition back in my first year in college. Now I was attending an Episcopal church near campus. Certainly part of that decision was some form of rebellion, but I had found in that place a freshness to the gospel and an approach to worship that invigorated what had been a dying spirituality. All of which intrigued my father. He grew up a Lutheran but traced his spiritual journey back to a conversion experience in his early twenties at Moody Church in Chicago. Talk of a sacramental approach to church and to the whole of life brought back those memories of Swedish Lutheranism in the U.P.

Not surprisingly, this new spiritual connection between us got off to a lurching start. Usually during Sunday dinners after several moments of the usual quiet, he would blurt out something like, "But what about infant baptism, what's your justification?"

"You mean, what about the Bible, right?"

"I mean, what's your justification?"

"Who needs justification?" I would say, sounding like I had been an Anglican from birth. "The church has been doing it for centuries!"

"That doesn't make it right."

And off we went meandering through biblical and theological issues for the rest of the afternoon. Both Mom and Dad began attending that Anglo-Catholic parish where I had been a member for a couple of years. Dad insisted on reading all he could find about Anglicanism. He borrowed a prayer book and hymnal from the church so he could understand as much as he could about what I was doing.

Although our communication continued to improve, I was not surprised to discover more about his spiritual journey through what he wrote rather than what he said. After completely making the switch to the Episcopal church he was asked to write a chapter in a book about evangelicals converting to Anglicanism. I was amazed by what I read in the chapter—and delighted. Dad was becoming my friend; a soul- friend.

Not long after my graduation from college, he was suddenly inspired to write the last of his Sebastian novels. The time that had lapsed after the fifth in that series was longer than the gaps between any of the others, and it was overdue. Whether or not he realized his time was short (I suspect he did), he decided that the research could not be done alone. He invited me to travel with him to Australia. Now, of course, I cherish that trip like a rare jewel. We had never spent time alone like that. The experience of watching him research a novel—especially a sea chase plot—is still one of the many shining facets of our time "down under." Sailing the South Pacific, working our way up the eastern coast of Australia, we talked like adults. We shared our dreams about life. By this time I had read all his books, and we talked about plot lines and character development. We discussed the impact a story can make and the power of the written word to change lives. I shared with him, for the first time, my sense of calling to the ministry.

It should not have surprised any of us when I began talking about seminary. The newfound freshness of the gospel that had been planted in college was beginning to blossom. Before I knew what was happening I was taking the first steps on the same path my own father had taken. Going away to seminary was really my first time *away* from home. Though our telephone conversations were frequent enough, Dad and I discovered a new level of bonding between us in the form of long letters. Although an outstanding preacher and inspiring teacher, the typewriter was the best way he knew how to communicate with his son. It bothered me some at first, but I realize now just how appropriate that was. His life was words —written words—and he knew no better way to share that life with me. His ability to breathe his imagination, his passionate spirit, into typed symbols on a page has left me living tokens of a man who believed the world could be changed with a pen.

How astounded I was to have all of this go churning through me, flashing through my memory with every spurt of adrenaline as I sped along that country road back in June 1987. I thought of Father's Day, just past, and how I wished I had been able to say on the phone what I had written on his card: "You know I love you, Dad. But I am also proud to be your son." I thought of his last letter in which he wrote that his only prayer back in the late 1970s had been that he would see me graduate from high school; then that God would allow him to see my degree from Wheaton College. How he looked forward to my seminary graduation and ordination next spring!

The news which greeted me at the end of that midnight journey may have been expected, but it was devastating nonetheless. The swiftness of his passing was indeed merciful for him but shattering for those left behind, who always have one more thing they want to say, one last token to offer of the bond that, even for a writer, transcends words. And then the panic. I was asked to offer a few of those transcendent words at his memorial service. I had to find words! The son of an author and teacher, I had to find some way to express in words what this man's life, dedicated to words, had meant to me.

To no one's amazement, Dad had planned his own memorial service in some detail. He also wanted several of his colleagues to talk about that consuming passion he called writing, that tireless energy he gave to teaching, and that gospel which drove him in all of it. My task? To speak from the perspective of a son.

After listening to the others speak that afternoon in the Barrows Auditorium (oddly reminiscent of the last time I heard testimonials in that building), I stood up with knees knocking and offered what I could:

What does a son say about his father?

We have already heard so much about what Jim Johnson has done. I suppose this means I must now somehow capture who he was as a father.

We would like to think that there exists some ideal father/son relationship out there; an ideal that we can work at and strive for. And then we fight with so much guilt after one of us dies because we think we did not strive hard enough or work long enough on that relationship.

But that is a myth.

No such ideal exists.

But what does exist, if I can call it this, is a mystical bond; a bond of creating and nurturing, a bond of flesh and spirit. We cannot describe it with words, nor does it always feel very good or manifest itself in exactly the way we would like.

So, in these many remembrances we have heard, what will I remember about my father?

In his "Last Word," printed in your programs, he left me a portion of poetry by Alfred Lord Tennyson:

> Not of the sunlight,
> Not of the moonlight,
> Not of the starlight!
> O young Mariner,
> Down to the haven,
> Call your companions,
> Launch your vessel,
> And crowd your canvass,
> And, ere it vanishes
> Over the margin,
> After it, follow it,
> Follow the Gleam.

I will remember the Gleam he left me; the gift of creativity—the will to dream, the yearning to write, the search for Truth led by the imagination. And I shall remember it in his laughter, his discipline, his heart, his gentleness.

What else will I remember about my father?

The struggles. Our struggle to understand each other. Our struggle to communicate. His struggle between being with his family and wielding the many gifts God had given him.

The struggle to learn to say, "I love you."

I thank God for these last nine years. Since his surgery we have learned and discovered so much about ourselves and each other. He quoted from another poem in those last words of his, a poem by Dylan Thomas:

> Do not go gentle into that good night,
> Old age should burn and rave at close of day;
> Rage, rage against the dying of the light.
>
> Though wise men at their end know dark is right,
> Because their words had forked no lightning they
> Do not go gentle into that good night.

Well, Dad, your words have forked lightning for me and for many others. And although I don't know what to say about the bond that we had and still have, I am glad I learned to say, "I love you." But what I needed to say, and what to say now, Dad, is that I am proud to be your son. I am so proud of you.

Now that I am serving as an Episcopal parish priest, something Dad longed to see, I sit back in awe as I watch my life take such ironic turns. I have just completed applications for postgraduate work in religious studies with the hope of one day teaching and writing. That which I vowed in anger never to consider, all that had driven my father, I am now striving to become.

On the November Sunday when we celebrated the Feast of All Saints, I was again reminded of those many discussions my father and I had about the Anglican tradition. He had some trouble with the notion of "saints," being unable to distinguish a legitimate remembrance of those whose example in life offers us hope in our own Christian journeys, and the abuse of that remembrance in the idea of "praying to a saint." We used to talk around that issue for hours.

I listened to our Sunday School students sing a delightful children's hymn, while memories of my father came flooding back, especially during the first verse:

> I sing a song of the saints of God
> patient and brave and true,
> Who toiled and fought and lived and died
> for the Lord they loved and knew.
> And one was a doctor and one was a queen
> and one was a shepherdess on the green:
> They were all of them saints of God—
> and I mean, God helping, to be one too.

Saints are not remembered as saints because they were somehow better than the rest of us; I can think of no more futile exercise. Rather, saints are remembered for being living "windows" through which we all can see the coming kingdom of God a little more clearly; windows through which we can see the passion of God with just a little more intensity; windows through which our journey home is slightly more illumined. A saint, I have discovered, can be a storyteller, the son of a potato farmer.

Seeing through the window of his life, I find myself following the same gospel-light that set his soul on fire. Through that window I can see a bit more clearly that Gleam and the journey of writing and teaching that just might bring me closer to home.

Leafing through Dad's books recently I found a dedication that reads, "To my son, Jay, whose great spirit is in this book." That spirit was his. By some unimaginable grace, he has passed it on.

James L. Johnson:
A Chronology

2-26-27   Born to Eric and Anna (Backman) Johnson
in Dollar Bay, Michigan

1939   Writes first short story at 12 years of age

1942   Stringer for *Houghton Gazette* (Michigan)
at 15 years of age

1944   Graduation from Dollar Bay High School,
Dollar Bay, Michigan

1945-46   Naval Service: World War II,
petty officer 3d class

1947-48   Suomi College, Hancock, Michigan
(two-year college)

1949   Begins work as dispatcher with
shipping company in Chicago

1951   Becomes a Christian

6-7-52   Marries Rosemary Lorts

1954-55   Student at Moody Bible Institute
            in Chicago, Illinois

1956-58   Missionary editor with Sudan Interior
            Mission (SIM), Nigeria, West Africa

1958   Returns to the United States for study

1959   Reenters Moody Bible Institute

1959-61   Pastor of the Elm-LaSalle Street Bible Church,
            Chicago, Illinois

1960   Graduates from Moody Bible Institute

            Is ordained

1961   Attends the University of Michigan, Ann Arbor

9-27-61   Son, Jay Emerson, is born

1963   Graduates from University of Michigan
            with B.A. in journalism

            Receives McNaught Award from the
            University of Michigan "for excellence
            in editorial writing"

            Becomes executive director of Evangelical
            Literature Overseas (ELO), Wheaton, Illinois

1967   First novel, *Code Name Sebastian*,
            published by J. B. Lippincott

1968   Starts Graduate School of Communications
            at Wheaton College, Wheaton, Illinois

Serves as chairman of the Communications
Commission of the World Evangelical
Fellowship

1970   Honored as Alumnus of the Year,
             Suomi College, Hancock, Michigan

1974   Receives Campus Life magazine's award,
             "Mark of Excellence, Poetry and Fiction,"
             for *The Death of Kings,* a novel

             Boston University requests he deposit his
             literary papers in their literary archives

1978   Major bypass surgery

1979   Returns to Evangelical Literature Overseas
             (ELO)

             Coming Back is published by Spring House

1982   Resigns from ELO to become Associate
             Executive Director for Resource Development
             at World Relief, Wheaton, Illinois

1983   Receives the Sherwood E. Wirt Award
             "for outstanding service to Christian writing"
             given by *Decision* Magazine School of Christian
             Writing

             Receives a Wheaton College Award
             from trustees, faculty, and students for
             "faithfulness to the vision that God gave you
             for a Graduate Communications Program"

Award of Recognition from Evangelical
Literature Overseas (ELO)

1985   Joins James F. Engel and Robert B. Reekie
          to form Media Associates International, Inc.
          (MAI), Bloomingdale, Illinois

1985-87   Director and officer of MAI
          from May 1985 until his death

6-25-87   Died on June 25, four months after
          his 60th birthday

Other Memberships and Honors:

Sigma Delta Chi, professional journalism society

Life member, Kappa Tau Alpha journalism
     society, "for outstanding editorial
     achievement"

Honorary member, Mark Twain Society

Authors' Guild

Listing in *Who's Who in Contemporary Authors
     in the Midwest*

Books by
James L. Johnson

Fiction

Sebastian Series

Code Name Sebastian	1967	Lippincott
Nine Lives of Alphonse	1968	Lippincott
A Handful of Dominoes	1970	Lippincott
A Piece of the Moon Is Missing	1970	Holman
The Last Train from Canton	1981	Zondervan
Trackless Seas	1987	Crossway

Other Novels

The Death of Kings	1974	Doubleday
The Tender Summer	1985	Harvest House

Nonfiction

The Nine to Five Complex	1972	Zondervan
Before Honor	1975	Holman
What Every Woman Should Know About a Man	1977	Zondervan
Loneliness Is Not Forever	1979	Moody
Coming Back	1979	Springhouse
How to Enjoy Life and Not Feel Guilty	1980	Harvest House

Retitled and Reprinted in Paperback

Scars and Stripes (*Before Honor*)	1981	Harvest House
All the King's Men (*The Death of Kings*)	1981	Harvest House
Profits, Power and Piety (*Nine to Five Complex*)	1980	Harvest House
First Four Sebastian Series (in paperback carton)	1978	Zondervan

Foreign Translations

Code Name Sebastian	1970	German
Code Name Sebastian	1977	Spanish
What Every Woman Should Know About a Man	1982	German
Loneliness Is Not Forever	1985	Chinese

"The Last Word"
and Other Articles

That Way-Out Ideal

Excerpt from 1969 article by Jim Johnson
Moody Monthly, *July/August 1969*

What you need in a woman is a combination of Miss America, Whistler's mother, Florence Nightingale, Abbie van Buren, and Agatha Christie"—in other words, beauty, maternal instinct, nursing ability (for my hypochondriac tendencies), counselor, and writer.

In other words, man, a way-out ideal!

The friend who jokingly suggested these ingredients for me was not too far out, for such specifications were pretty much lined up with my needs. As a non-Christian, steeped in chronic alcoholism, I had some real psychological problems. I was trying to meet those needs in drink and the general hell-bent-for-leather philosophy of life that goes with a man running scared.

Then I came to know Christ and most of my psychological needs were met in Him. But I still carried that "ideal woman" image with me. In fact, my stubborn conception of her almost lost me the perfect ideal God had in mind.

I remember seeing Rosemary for the first time across a crowded room. It was in a large church at the beginning of a missionary conference. I was only six weeks old in the Lord, still recovering from a wild life of dissipation and still bearing the marks of dereliction. I recall that people were kind to me, but I wasn't much to get next to, as far as the girls were concerned. I looked pretty much like something the cat dragged in.

But seeing Rosemary that evening, I felt a peculiar awareness that this might just be the one girl tailor-made to fulfill my way-out ideals. Maybe it was just an impulse, but it was enough to get me on the pursuit.

But how was I to approach her? As a new Christian, I was still pretty much on the defensive about my past. Did I just walk up to her and say, "The Lord gave me an impulse about you"?

No. I knew that interpersonal relationships, even in the family of God, had to be on a sounder basis than that. Somehow I would have to find God's leading in the situation. So, not having the nerve to foist my bedraggled self on her, I let the opportunity slip, telling God it was up to Him to do it.

God arranged the first contact that week. At the conference she was in charge of guiding people through the African display booth. It was an imitation of a hut where you walked in and viewed symbols representing the spiritual darkness of another world. When my turn came to go in, she appeared as my guide. Since it was a dimly lighted place I didn't get to see much of her. But one thing I liked—the tone of her voice, not authoritative like a UN guide, but warm and friendly. She was concerned that I might personally get the full impact of the display.

I believe God arranged that contact in just that way—in the dimness of that exhibit—that I might catch the voice, the personality revealed in her tone, the inflection of her words, the quiet, gentle spirit of her life. Why so important? Because I knew I couldn't take a sharply authoritative, all knowing, domineering quality to begin with—somehow God knew that my makeup demanded a quiet, sensitive type of person. I didn't realize it fully at the time, but this was the first big step toward a relationship God had in mind for me eons ago.

If You Are Real, Take Over

The following is Jim Johnson's own story of
his life-changing decision to follow Jesus Christ
on February 15, 1951. Jim wrote these words based on
a vivid flashback just moments before he underwent
radical quadruple open heart bypass surgery in 1978.
The excerpt here is from chapter 3 of his book
Coming Back, *published in 1979.*
Used by permission of Harvest House.

I remembered the first pain back in 1970 while
heading for a gate at O'Hare Airport. It came on me like indi-
gestion, a sharp burning, yet grabbing pain. I tried to believe
it was due to the quick hotdog I had eaten in the terminal.
But as I walked, the pain grew until it was a fist trying to shut
off my breath. I stopped and waited. I was perspiring. The
garment bag in my left hand felt like cement. My attache case
in my right hand felt like an anvil. I put them down and
leaned my two hands on the rail. I had no fright. It was "just
one of those things." After a few minutes the pain subsided,
and I went on to make connections. Two days later I felt a
slight twinge on the way back out of O'Hare.

It was the beginning, the warning. The heart was starting
to labor under the stress of clogging plaques in the arteries. I
didn't know that. I didn't want to know. I had things to do. To
me it was no more than a pesky corn on the toe. In time it
would settle down. Cut out the onions and garlic.

If I had known it was the beginning of a growing crisis
"inside," I probably would not have stopped anyway. Yet way
back then God was blowing the whistle on me, trying to get
my attention. Ignoring God's signals about the stress on the
body has killed better men than me. But don't we always figure we can lick anything that comes? For me, illness had always been a bout with the flu or dyspepsia. I had been
around the world three times and survived. I could keep doing it. The pride of man is fanatical. It is also akin to a sin
against the body—even against God.

My mind shifted to Dollar Bay, Michigan, up near Lake Superior, a town of no more than 1,500 people. It was a mill town tucked between two hills, sitting on a lagoon leading to Portage Lake. People worked the mills and grew potatoes, drank gallons of coffee a day and let the world go by. I remembered the depression, the empty larder, the lines to pick up a sack of flour, sugar, some canned horse meat and dried prunes . . . the cold winters when the wind blew through thin walls, when the thermometer dropped to 36 below, and the snow in one night piled up more than six feet.

Yet it was a comfortable place to live. The Depression drew the six of us in the family together. We patched old clothes to wear to school. We made taffy and had a celebration just pulling the stuff into shape. Life was tough, but a spirit grew then, and there was love.

The lazy summer when I was 14 I rowed a boat out of the lagoon onto the lake, going nowhere in particular but loving the water and the sun and life bursting inside. A friend sat in the back smoking a cigarette, ragweed rolled in Montgomery Ward catalogue paper.

"What'ya gonna do when you grow up?" he asked, puffing.

"I dunno. What are you?" The water slurped under the bow as I pulled on the oars.

"Science . . . I'm gonna make things in test tubes."

"Why that?"

"Some day I'll produce a man out of a test tube."

I laughed. "You can't even make zinc oxide in chemistry class," I reminded him.

"So what?" His eyes glazed as he puffed on the "Montgomery Ward special." "Anybody can make zinc oxide. Some day I'll hit one for the fences. Wait." One day he would be connected with a big chemical corporation. He was sure of himself even then.

"So I told you . . . what about you?" he prodded me. I didn't answer, so he said, "I bet I know . . . you'll probably write the great American novel." I laughed.

"Don't be nuts."

"You don't think I know you sneak into the high school typing room after you clean up and type out those stories?" he asked. I was uncomfortable. I had done that. I had waited for Saturdays to let my imagination run. They had no form or substance, but I wrote stories. Westerns. Sports stories where I carried the ball for touchdowns. I wrote for the sheer pleasure of seeing words on paper.

"Remember that baseball story you wrote?" he asked. "I remember that great line . . . 'The batter hit a screaming liner that trickled through Locatelli's legs.' I like that. A screaming liner trickling through anybody's legs is a bit of a do." And he laughed, coughing on his ragweed.

"Cut it out," I mumbled. I rowed the boat harder, embarrassed.

"But you sure wrote a beaut of an essay for me in English," he added, his voice now respectful. "I mean, did you hear old lady LeBlanc rave over my great prose? Maybe I shoulda told her it was yours. But she raves over you every day. Yup, I just bet you're gonna write books, lots of books . . . you can tell a story better'n Hemingway."

"What do you know about Hemingway?"

"I read. Required reading in English, remember? I like the way you tell stories better."

We rowed on, and I was uneasy. Nobody talked writing to me. In this town survival was based on getting into the mills or plowing a straight row for potatoes. I also wrote secretly in longhand on lined pads of paper at home. I wrote poems about war and blood, because Germany was arming and hitting places like Poland and Czechoslovakia. I wrote about loneliness.

My father had been in a sanitarium for most of my growing up years. I had to find my way as best I could, leaning on my older brothers, Nelson, Larry, and Thurston, whom we called "Toast." They did their best to give me the masculine guidance I needed. But it was never quite enough. So my writing became a way to air my feelings.

When I thought of the future, I was scared. I didn't have my act together. Only when I made the basketball team in my sophomore year did I feel I had ratified something of worth in me. That had only come after horrendous hours of practicing on lumpy winter outdoor courts, in below zero temperatures. I nearly froze my fingers shooting one-handers, developing the long two-hand shot of those days. I had to do something well early in life if I was going to make it at all. Maybe that's what started the hypertension in the first place—the need to excel to prove something about myself.

Getting drunk was another rite of passage. I was in the bars as early as 16. It was wartime. The age limits were hedged. We were young men soon to face it ourselves. I didn't mind. Fighting like Audie Murphy blazing away at the enemy wasn't so bad. And getting drunk was a means of being something I was not.

Then, the navy. Drill, discipline, reveille, obstacle courses, firing ranges. It was 1944, and I was getting ready to be a hero. My first night on the Landing Ship Tank in San Diego was in a repair yard covered with hoses and lines and garbage. Nobody met me on the quarter deck. The two sailors on watch were fast asleep. Was this my stage for heroism?

I walked around the cluttered decks and found myself at the anti-aircraft gun forward. Looking at the twin barrels, I wondered what it was going to be like firing at an enemy plane. The lights of San Diego were shining brightly. The war was a long way off. I stood there and created poetry about guns and lights, and the stink of garbage and grease.

At sea I was made Storekeeper/Yeoman. I made Petty Office Third in three months. I could have made First, but I spent my time at the typewriter in the office writing short stories about the sea, the ship, the battles I imagined yet to come. One piece got to the captain, and he called me in.

"You're kind of different, Johnson," he said.

Not again. Was I an oddball or what? I waited.

"I like your writing. I'm going to send it to *Stars and Stripes*. How'd you like to do a ship's paper? Kind of pick up the morale for the crew?"

Horrors! I didn't want to be reduced to being the "ship's scribe." I wanted "battle stations"! I wanted to stand my watches in the night with the rest.

"Cut your watches and give attention to a ship's paper. That's an order."

My dreams of being another Audie Murphy were gone. I wrote about other sailors in battle above decks. I wrote jokes. I wrote about "Dear John" letters that the crew had received and answered some for them. I wrote about beaches running with blood and bravery beyond what I had ever known. I got drunk with them on liberty. I found something with them that I had never experienced, even though I was "the scribbler" to them. I have never again known the unity like that which binds men in war. I needed it. It was my bridge to manhood.

"Why don'ya write about colored people?"

"Like what?"

"Like look at me . . . Chestnut . . . I'm a commissary steward . . . tha's all I ever be! We colored folks stay in one compartment, separate from whites. We stand the watches, some get shot at, too. But we got to be separate. Why don'ya write about that?"

"I wouldn't know what to say about that. It's military policy."

"Yea . . . man . . . well, God knows . . . you know anything about God, Johnson?"

"I had the catechism, sure, in the Lutheran church. I grew up in that church. Sure, I know about God."

"But you ain't known Him yet like a friend, right?"

"Friend? God is out there, Chestnut. You don't bring Him down out of the universe to cuddle with."

He laughed as if he had something secret. "You gonna write some things, Johnson . . . lots a'things . . . maybe you be famous some day, and I can say I knew ya . . . but you need to know God as a friend first. You is as empty as me, know that? No . . . you is as empty as I was. You don't have no respect of persons, color or nothin'. You get Him close to ya, and you gonna write something some day that means something . . . "

The typhoon came. Moments of wet terror. Black-green waves rose 20 feet over our 420-foot LST that never should have sailed into a frog pond—let alone open sea—during a typhoon. She rolled sickeningly, each time seeming to go over farther and threatening never to come back. I stood with five other crew members in the galley, hanging on to a stanchion for dear life. Every time the ship went over in a huge swell, we yelled in fright.

In the middle of it my left shoulder banged into the bulkhead. The steel-plated New Testament was in my shirt pocket. I had never read it. Someone had sent it from home in a Christmas box. I liked the steel cover. I took it to battle stations figuring no shrapnel could hit me in the left ventricle with that protection. Now I felt for it, took it out, hunted in the index for "fear" and found Psalm 91. Thank God somebody had the foresight to index that important word!

I flipped to it and read the verse, "Though a thousand fall at thy side and ten thousand at thy right hand, it shall not come nigh thee. . . ." I could hear the voices of captains from other ships over the TBS (Talk Between Ships) yelling that they were going down. Bigger ships. So I shouted the verse to the terrified men around me. Then, in no more than five minutes, the rage of the storm ceased. We stood flat, staring at one another. We had come into the eye of the storm. I was still standing there, my New Testament open. The rest of them were staring at me . . .

"You want to come?" Ray said.

"Look, I'm not interested . . . I'm not sure of this Moody kind of religion. I got a date later anyway . . . "

"So try it," he insisted. He and I had grown up together, played basketball together. He was a clean-cut, athletic type. A month before he had told me he had "accepted Christ." I got mad. I told him he was stupid to swallow all that. He was the only real friend I had in Chicago. This was 1951, February 15. I was just barely hanging on in a job with a shipping company, all of $41.00 per week. My writing wasn't going anywhere. I was drinking more to find some of that old "bravado." I hated to turn Ray down. I liked him. He was a link to survival in some way.

"Okay, so I'll try it . . . but nobody better touch me about religion or conversion, Okay?"

So I found myself in that huge cavern called Moody Church Auditorium that seats 4,000 people. I figured I could be anonymous in that place. I wasn't ignorant of what was to come. I remembered Isaac Franz, my neighbor in Dollar Bay, an old man as I grew up who preached Christ day in and day out. I had gotten some of that, because the piano was playing hymns across the yard almost every day. From my bedroom, coming out of a hangover, I could hear it clearly enough. His son, Herb, also a kind of wild drinking Swede, was converted himself only a few years back. He had won Ray and his wife, June, to the Lord a couple of months ago. I was aware of the "pitch" that was to come. I put my defenses up and prepared to do battle. I didn't want religion to come in and destroy my writing dreams. I didn't want any complication now, anything that might steer me away from what I had to do.

Yet something was right about this place. Though I didn't want to get "hooked" in this "Moody stuff," there was nothing "peculiar" or "wrong" about Ray. So the fight went on. I remembered Chestnut who said, "Take God as your friend." I thought of my life's uncertainties, meaninglessness, failure, and a future that promised little. I thought of my drab youth filled with so much insecurity, fear, loneliness. I needed love, someone to care. I was 25 years old. It was a time in life when a man had to face himself or go under.

The preacher's name was Dr. Franklin S. Logsdon. His sermon title was "Where Will the Sinful and Ungodly Be?" I didn't hear much of his message. I felt only the battle within me. I figured in the end God had to be better than what I had. There had to be a better future in Him than what I was heading into. If Chestnut were right, then maybe now was the time.

When the invitation came, I went forward to the prayer room. It was not a good prayer I spoke. No theology in it, no familiar church language. I didn't know any of that. I just asked Christ, "If You are real, then take over and make something of me." I didn't ask Him to make me a great writer, to fulfill my dreams. I just asked Him to start some reconstruction. And He did.

I didn't understand all that had happened to me, but I knew when I went out of that huge church that I was somebody else. "God the Friend" was in my life. I knew why Chestnut laughed now with so much delight in his "secret."

Now I knew I was going to make it, to be something for Somebody . . . at last, I knew.

The Power of Fiction

An article written in 1981 by Jim Johnson
© 1981 by Interlit, *David C. Cook Foundation,*
Elgin, Illinois 60120
Reprinted with permission

When Eugene Burdick and Robert Lederer finished their manuscript *The Ugly American* some years back, it was pure documentary—that is, a factual account of the tragic mistakes of American foreign policy in Asia. But after the manuscript had already been accepted by the publisher and moving to typesetting stage, so the story goes, both authors came to the same conclusion: change that book from a documentary to a novel. And they did. (The publisher almost fainted!)

Why did they? Because the authors realized that drama has immense power to take the *facts* of experience and heighten them to compelling dimensions the reader never forgets.

Of course, there is credence for the nonfiction book, the documentary, and the expositional. These do an important service of providing information. But Anne Glossack had it right in her article "Why Fiction?" (published in *Writer Magazine,* 1976) when she said, "It should be pointed out that an even greater impact can be produced on the reader's mind by showing him in story form, just what these facts, memoirs, beliefs, and theories can mean in *human terms.*"

The Ugly American proved to be a classic, because it provided a story with all the elements of character, suspense, plot, and dialogue while never losing the factual level of the theme.

One reason why writers who are Christian do not go with fiction more often (or perhaps the publisher is more reticent) is that they believe that fiction is for entertainment and escapism. Therefore, it is a form that seems beneath the "calling" of the composer. But supposing *Moby Dick,* Herman Melville's classic novel, had been done as a purely theological treatise on the theme of "vengeance is mine, saith the Lord"? Would Melville have captured the imagination of readers even to this time in history if it had been done that way? Probably not. My opinion is that Melville decided that the theology lesson could be best communicated through fiction, through a vengeful Captain Ahab, an uncertain and fearful crew, and the whale himself, Moby Dick.

Entertainment and escapism as motives are not wrong if within that there is also the maintaining of the purpose—to communicated Truth. Leslie Conger in her column in *The Writer* magazine (July 1981) commented on this by saying, "C. S. Lewis once said that escapism is a dirty word only to those who are by instinct jailers." And when Emily Dickinson wrote, "There is no frigate like a book, to take us lands away" surely she was writing in approval of the trip.

"And," she adds, "Each of us is confined by whatever life we lead, for no life is totally unbounded; and most of us feel the want of an occasional boarding pass to a frigate which will take us somewhere else."

Anne Glossack supports this by stating, "Thanks to the storybooks I have wept beside a dying King Arthur, stood shoulder to shoulder with d'Artagnan, and climbed the rigging of a ship of the line with Captain Horatio Hornblower. It is fiction that beguiles us into burrowing beneath the skin of another person and trying a different life-style on for size."

But in providing this journey for the reader, the writer who is Christian has a distinct task at hand: to make that "way out" journey, with its drama about mankind's struggles, hopes, defeats, and victories, an opportunity to amplify the image of God within our experiences.

Consider the power of Lew Wallace's biblical novel *Ben Hur*, especially in terms of how the Crucifixion changed the lives of the main characters. Or again, Lloyd Douglas's *The Robe*, which showed what two people went through in dedicating their lives to Christ during the height of the Roman Empire.

No, the writer should not step back from fiction as something "lesser" in terms of communicating Christ. Some one has aptly said that it is art in the end that endures.

And yet, though many writers believe this, their problem in facing into fiction is in terms of how to develop it properly. Indeed, if there is one glaring shortcoming that characterizes much fiction written by Christians it is the shallowness of story, the superficiality of the characters, and the emptiness and irrelevance of the plot.

And yet there are writers who have managed to master the craft of fiction, some because of a natural gift for the art form, and for others (many others) by being exposed to how the parts are drawn and how they work together. For example: Dostoevski, Tolstoy, Graham Greene, and Flannery O'Connor.

Given, then, the fact that fiction is a powerful tool in terms of the dramatic impact, the issue comes down to facing the major parts that go into a good novel or short story. Where does fiction begin? With character, situation, conflict—what or which? Or maybe they all come together at once? How important is the character to the story? How does one balance the development of character against the need for sustaining suspense and complication of plot line?

Everyone has one good story to tell . . . some have dozens. One must believe it is worth telling first of all. Then one must mix the ingredients properly to make it believable and compelling.

. . . fear of being swallowed up by the anonymity of the Arctic Sea . . .
And All for the Sake of Reality

By Jim Johnson
Published in Moody Monthly, *October 1975*

*I*t was 72 degrees below zero.

I hopped from one foot to the other, despite heavy fur-lined boots and three pairs of socks: despite 10 pounds or more of outer clothing plus heavy thermal underwear, fur lined trousers, and a heavy fleece lined lumberjack shirt. On top of that was a bulky parka, lined with wolverine fur, and a hood that encased my face. My hands, wrapped in two layers of woolen mittens with an outer pair of insulated leather, still felt like clubs.

I kept telling myself the Arctic was no place for a temperate Swede who never remembered it ever getting lower than 25 below in the lumber towns of Upper Michigan where I grew up; and in the last ten years I hadn't known anything close to that in the central heat of Wheaton, Illinois. But here I was doing an Irish jig on Arctic ice that rumbled like it wanted to belch up half the world right under my feet.

Two Eskimos moved in a blur of cold and snow as they put up the yellow vinyl tents and tied down the dog teams. The sun was gone now. A macabre darkness came down on the ice. This was March 6, only a week after the official calendar termination of the six months of winter when the sun never came up. Today the sun had come up for only a few hours, a pinkish ball that cast a weird pallor, turning the empty landscape of ice into a Disneyland of kaleidoscopic wonder. But then all too suddenly, it slid off its climbing track and sank below the horizon as if someone had shot a hole in it.

I crawled into the tent, my teeth chattering. The air force sergeant, my official guide, lit the primus. Yellow, saffron light filled the tent making our eyes dilate in the wonder of it. I was never going to get warm again, I was sure of that, regardless of the primus stove faithfully hissing an uncertain promise. The two Eskimos, who would sleep in the other tent, unpacked our boxes. The pots came out first, and one of the Eskimos scooped snow into a pan from the outside of the tent. There were traces of dog urine in it, but they paid no attention and put it on the stove to melt.

I gulped. I'd been gulping for two days now. My spit was continually thick from the fear I felt—fear of being swallowed up by the black anonymity of the Arctic Sea that showed its ugly backside to me every time ice broke open and pushed a wide chasm of ten feet or more, fear of the wind that came from those long plains of never-ending ice, and razor sharp snow that slashed open facial skin and left its scars of frost bite that burned long into the night as they thawed in the tent; fear of a storm that would maroon us, the food running out, the radio failing and never being able to make contact with rescue back on the mainland of Greenland.

With all my clothes on I crawled into my sleeping bag, hoping for warmth to penetrate the deadness of my frozen legs and arms and hands, staring up into the shadows cast against the tent roof. One of the Eskimos handed me a clump of the gray stuff they called "pemmican," which was seal blubber that smelled like a combination of a dead cat and castor oil.

I tried a smile that didn't do anything to my frozen lips and cheeks and shook my head.

"Eat! Good!" Eskimo Charlie said to me, his brown, smoke lined face bending over me, small yellow teeth gleaming in the light. "Make you *Innuit!*"

Innuit is the Eskimo word for man. Well, if pemmican was to make a man of me, I opted to stay a child. I had about run out of true grit after only two days in these elements, the tent walls flapping in the wind, the ice rumbling its continual threats, and the everlasting smell of pemmican driving a steak-and-potato stomach to sheer trepidation.

So, now, again, I asked myself the question I had asked a dozen times in my writing career: *Is this trip really necessary?* I was here to try to get some "reality of the Arctic" for my fourth Sebastian novel, *A Piece of the Moon is Missing.* As with all my books, I make it a point to visit the locale where I set the story. Each trip unquestionably did something for my writing, but each also ended with me inside my sleeping bag protecting myself from some real or imagined crisis. In the blistering Negev Desert south of Palestine, chasing through the free Cuban communities in Miami, or cruising through the lifeless streets of East Berlin, I had to ask myself honestly if this was the only way to get reality into my novels.

I thought of the warm, comfortable library back in Wheaton that could give me all I needed to know about Arctic temperatures and storms and ice drifts, survival kits, Eskimo dogs, the whole bit.

Why did I feel I had to go through all this—to taste, smell, hear and half die just to put together a piece of fiction for readers who might not care one way or the other if it was done on "location" or not? (People do care, I have found.)

And yet as I felt the rattle of the tent under the mounting gusts, I knew the answer. It was the answer I always got, even in other corners of the world doing the same kind of research. It was really the way Christ Himself would do it. He had already demonstrated the only way to bring reality. He proved, as I had to learn, that reality does not grow on trees, nor can it be plucked from some library list.

If that was the case, then God could have stayed in the "stack room" in Heaven and programmed redemption on the card index that held all the secrets of the universe. But redemption could not be accomplished by the numbers, a few thousand miles out of the action. John 1:14 says that "The Word became flesh and dwelt among us, and we beheld His glory, the glory of the only begotten of the Father, full of grace and truth." Could Jesus have accomplished redemption by simply being vaporous spirit, hanging a few safe miles above the smog of humanity, perhaps using a bull horn and shouting, "Thus saith the Lord"?

There were times when His disciples figured it could be done that way, even as I did in my lonely, frostbitten hours of research. When Jesus was transfigured on that mountain top, and all the glory that was His illuminated Him in awesome spectacle, and when Moses and Elias appeared with Him, it was then that Peter suggested: "Lord, let us build three churches up here . . . one for you, one for Moses and one for Elias . . ."

Peter's implied question really was not unlike the one a lot of Christians ask these days: "Is there any point in going back down to that valley anymore? We could have three churches up here; and once a week, Lord, we could advertise in the *Jerusalem Times* that you are going to turn on your transfiguration glory again, say on the Sabbath, and everybody could then come up here. We would never have to go back down, never have to face the crud, grime, dust, and heartbreak of that place . . ."

But the Lord saw through it. He was not interested in any real estate transactions on the mountain top. For Him, redemption could not be accomplished by the "up-up-and-away" mentality but only through deliberate identification with those who needed that redemption. Credibility was at stake, in other words, and if mankind was to ever give Him a second look in terms of what He said and did on the cross, then He had to suffer as they suffered, to know their trauma, the times of laughter, and the times of tears.

—And all for the sake of reality.

But now as the sergeant turned down the primus stove and blew out the tilly lamp, plunging the tent into gravelike darkness, I told God I was a pretty reluctant martyr and surely no hero. I knew Jesus was not bucking for the Hall of Fame either, but at least He has the legions of angels at His beck and call. Maybe it was time to "Make my calling—and election sure" rather than court the "short, happy life of one J. L. Johnson." Because all I had was the lousy taste of seal blubber in my mouth, a frost-bitten nose, a lump of fear around my heart, and a pretty thin frosting of humanity that wouldn't do much to sweeten death which could come at any second.

And yet I knew deep down that there was no other way to communicate Christ anywhere to any people, be they listeners or readers, unless there was something of reality in it all. I had to build bridges to readers who would judge me as any literary jury would, on the basis of how well I knew my locale, the people, their conflicts, before they would ever accept what I had to say about the concern of Christ for the lostness of those people.

Someone has said that good writing is 90 percent research and 10 percent writing. I am not so sure those ratios are accurate, but I do know that writing that impresses me is done by authors who know what they are writing about in every sense. I knew, even as the dogs howled into the frigid wind outside, that it was not enough to say I knew the Bible or all about redemption, the atonement, and the Second Coming, and at the same time admit my ignorance, in terms of experience, of the state of man to which these glorious words are intended.

Any man who really wants to can research on "location." Any Christian who wants to understand the totality of the people he is seeking to relate to for Christ—the emotional, physical, spiritual—can do so by taking time to listen to them, sympathize and observe. It's always easier to open a can of beans for unexpected guests than to take the time to find out what their tastes really are. Once this is evident, the effort put into the preparing and serving is worth it all.

So tomorrow, if God gave me the night, I would probably eat some of that seal blubber, looking straight into the eye of that Eskimo Charlie and pinching off the nose in my brain so my taster would be paralyzed. It was not courageous or noble, this "research," but to Charlie it was being a true *Innuit*. If I was going to talk about him in my book, I owed him that much. And to those readers who thought enough to honor me in imbibing my prose, I certainly owed them that much.

A Question of Antiseptics

*An unedited manuscript written by
James L. Johnson in the early sixties*

*I*t was in the middle of one of those church study commissions on "global outreach" that this "young whippersnapper" tossed the bomb.

We had been rolling along on the usual "weighty" matters of skid row missions, tract distribution, and beefing up the Easter cantata—and then we came to the planning of the contest with four other churches in the city as to who would bring the most people to Sunday School. It was then that this young Turk piped up with, "Why don't we compete to see who can get the most tins of powdered milk for the suffering children of Biafra?"

There followed that long period of silence that often comes in these groups when the goading matters of social conscience run the light and crack us in our spiritual solar plexus. Then came the uncomfortable word chewing session that stuck to our teeth like caramel until somebody shut it all off by saying, "The best thing to do for Biafrans is to get the Gospel to them as quickly as possible, since life seems so short for them . . ."

That was theologically accurate and clean, of course, but it fell considerably short of the issue. And yet I knew what that commission was going through, bouncing that rather hot potato around the room. I had faced it myself, ten years ago, as a missionary in Nigeria, dispensing the Gospel faithfully for every situation, until one day there was a confrontation. An African, who had his home destroyed by fire that left him and his family destitute, listened very politely to my careful exposition of the Gospel as the prognosis for his case, and said, "Thank you, sir . . . in the meantime my children are homeless . . . all our possessions are gone . . . can you help me until I can get on my feet again?"

And I hesitated. Why? Because my pre-conditioning for service was not in that direction. There was no bridge for me to cross over from a strictly spiritual compartment to a social one. I had received no orientation in the great Commission that said I actually had responsibility for feeding the hungry. That was a job for UNESCO or UNICEF or the World Relief Commission. But I know now that beyond my ignorance was the fact that I really didn't want to go beyond the clean and safe boundaries of word dispensing to the dirty business of works. (The Apostle James notwithstanding). But I thank God for the presence of mind He gave me at that crucial point in my missionary life, to reach out with uncertain and feeble hands to lift that man out of his social ash heap—the impact on him was profound. But even after that, I wondered if I had done right!

So I know what that study commission was fighting in the uncomfortable silence following the neat side-stepping (or not so neat) of the social question. But it would seem that this whole matter of cleavage to the antiseptics of spiritual theory as against the dirty involvement with the mess of reality might account for the paralysis of the church's outreach. It may be what's keeping us from turning loose the energies of the church to affect problems of world famine in terms of desalinization of water for irrigation, perfecting synthetic foods, and transforming swamp land into productive soil. It may be the reason for our not thinking of "global outreach" and missions in the larger dimension of man's total need.

And, too, it may be the reason why I find myself still trying to attack my own community's problems of divorce, drug addiction, and alcoholism with bigger Christmas programs, splashier in-group socials, and Sunday School merit badge contests.

The result of all this is much like someone said in "Television Age": "Our subways aren't safe, our streets aren't safe, our parks aren't safe—but under our arms we've got complete protection." In other words, there are times when the spiritual aerosol treatment won't stretch quite far enough.

So the lessons learned in that "global outreach" study commission are apparent. Certainly, as a thinking man charged by God to do just that, I may have to stop scrubbing up to do surgery on a mannequin. I will certainly have to stop simply being "one more to make a quorum" on these commissions and honestly force some grappling with the issues.

It will mean, of course, that I won't by-pass the Gospel or the preaching of it in favor of food dispensing or bandage rolling. But it will mean that I will have to discern what are the best methods to communicate the love of Christ in every situation—and to avoid, at all costs, the tendency to fall back on selected safety texts in the Bible to keep me out of the dirty end of things.

This may mean becoming an unpopular goad to the soft underbelly of church decision making—but it is on this that the church (and civilization?) advances. I know of no more respectable call of God than that.

My Heart for Editorial Work

*An unedited address prepared in 1965
by James L. Johnson for the Evangelical
Press Association Convention in Chicago*

*M*y dad said to me once, "A closed mouth gathers no foot."

He said that to me after my first experience of editing at the age of 13. I related this story to you last year at the EPA convention, and I am going to do it again because it sets the pace for much of what I've experienced since then.

When I was 13 and in my early adolescent years, three of us got together and decided to run the first newspaper for a little town called Dollar Bay, Michigan. We put it on 8 1/2 x 11 . . . found an old mimeograph that came from the junk yard . . . got it operative and some old paper that was smeared on the back but clear we thought on the front. And soon we began to run our first newspaper for a town of 1,400 people.

Trouble is it turned out to be an editorial harangue. We called the Lutheran minister a Communist because he took away our basketball club practice for confirmation classes. We didn't know what a Communist was, but it sounded pretty bad so we wanted to tag him with that.

We also went down the garden path against the fire chief who didn't flood our ice rink every week so we could have our hockey game as scheduled.

. . . And for the milkman who "upped" the price of our chocolate milk from five cents to seven cents and put us completely out of the market we also had a few words.

And so, this was our first newspaper. It didn't turn out to be news, however; it turned out to be all editorial, of course, and I made the mistake of having my name on it. The other two convinced me of this procedure, and I felt quite good about it. I was quite proud of the fact that I could turn out a thing like this with my name on it.

At five o'clock that wintry February afternoon we distributed this paper. Called it the *Dollar Bay Crusader* yet, and we hit every house in the place.

One hour afterward, sitting at supper, the news caught fire. The Lutheran minister wanted an immediate explanation, the fire chief practically cried over what I had said about him. The milkman said he couldn't help but raise the price, and the whole town was in a furor. To say the least we made a mild disturbance—so "mild," in fact, that I got scared, ran out of town, and spent three days in retreat in a hunting cabin. My family got so concerned about me they forgot about the furor. So that was my first experience of editing. That was when my dad said to me, "Son," very quietly and patiently and heaving a great sigh, "remember: A closed mouth gathers no foot."

I am a writer and very happy to be a writer, unless the editors want to fight about it. In 1956 I was sent as a writer to Lagos, Nigeria, West Africa. But, you can imagine my consternation when on arrival I was told as I entered the office that I was to be the editor . . . to replace Harold Fuller who had to go home on furlough.

Immediately all of the complications set in again, and I even told them this story of what happened to me as an editor in that little town of Dollar Bay. It didn't phase that mission board in the least. So I appealed to them and to the home board. I finally appealed to God where I should have gone in the first place. He said, "Stand still and see the glory of God." Eventually I did but not at first.

I didn't give them much in that first few months of editing the *Challenge*, but the job was mine, and this assignment for today said that I was supposed to say something on how editing gripped me.

Well, those first few months of editing *African Challenge* gripped a lot of people painfully, including myself. It "gripped" me, for instance, three months after my arrival when I heard that we got a 30,000-pound libel suit, of all things, for running a story on a man that was fiction. He said it was the actual story of his life, and we had made the mistake of not putting on there, "This story has no resemblance to persons living or dead." He had us cold. Gripped! We finally found a Christian lawyer who got us out of this.

The editorial work gripped me, too, when a fanatical Muslim responded to an article I cleared on the fruitlessness of sacrificing bulls and goats for remission of sins. He answered, "We will be glad to change this animal sacrifice at next Ramadan for your rich American blood." I got a little scared after that and wondered if I was really in the right position or not.

Editorial work also gripped me when a 6-foot 7-inch, 250 pound African Communist roared into my office one day carrying half the door frame with him. He wanted to protest the fact that I began a series of articles on communism by Tom Dooley entitled, "Deliver Us From Evil." That Communist was about to bury me alive.

Editorial work gripped me also the day I used an editorial with a photograph of a girl to illustrate an article titled "Immorality in Our Schools." There was another suit in the making. We never prayed so hard in our lives. We were "gripped" in the real sense of the word!

So my editorial life has been filled with precarious adventures in learning which is not the easiest way to break into print. You can break your pocketbook, too. Very often many of the things I have done were purely out of ignorance. Even though we must publish at our peril, there is no business that I know of in the Kingdom of God in which I find richer dividends.

The first of these dividends that God gave back in those hectic months when I had to edit a magazine was the matter of influence. That mimeographed paper I produced in that little town of Dollar Bay, of course, had a tremendous influence. That Lutheran minister never had so many people in his church at one time. They all flocked in there to see what a Communist looked like. That fire chief never missed a week of flooding the ice rink, and that milkman never dropped his price, but every noon he brought two cases of chocolate milk gratis for us to swallow.

So it was in Africa. Several times the *Challenge* was recognized by noted Nigerian publishers as an outstanding periodical. On one occasion an editor, in citing the magazine, said: "For courageous exposure of issues on true Christian morality in our history that has influenced our nation." I smiled at that, because really it was a blessed accident—at least when I was editing—although I knew the Lord was doing His blue penciling of my copy too.

I remember giving a commencement address at a technical college. I was introduced by the president who said, "We are proud to have the editor of a magazine willing to stand for Christian principles in an age when we seem to think that education is our God."

Oh, I think of many things of influence. Not only influence but inspiration. I think of the writers who got their start with a kind word given them. I remember getting a manuscript from a fellow in Africa written on the back of a shoe box cover—it was all he had—written there in nice ink. He started at the top and ended at the bottom, and I didn't know quite what he had said. But I looked at that and then wanted to throw it away. I said, "Wait a minute! This represents, per-haps, all the passion and desire and idealism of one writer." I wrote him back a full-page letter encouraging him. The next time he came back with some cheap onion skin which had been written on, and the paper had been so thin that it went all the way through, and I couldn't read a thing. So I sent him another letter. That writer today is writing one of our feature articles and is involved 100 per cent in Christian writing for various Christian periodicals.

I think of the inspiration of letters to editors. Some are humbling, but I think of correspondents who responded say-ing that they received help. I remember one letter I received after I had written an editorial on "The Evil of One Man's Tyr-anny." One man replied, "You are wrong, but I appreciate the fact that you had the guts to write it."

So editorial work in itself has influence and inspiration, and I found that in all these years I have had to learn the hard way and stumble through and go through all the agony of saying "I wonder if I can get by with this without hurting somebody."

Nevertheless, I have found that God in His leading and directing has brought great dividends. I leave you with three things with which God has blessed me and has taught me as an editor. One is *conviction*. No wishy-washy, in-between middle-of-the-road belief. Either you've got it, and you're ready to say it, or you don't say anything.

Secondly, *compassion*. Compassion for the writer who writes and who perhaps may not make the grade. A compas-sion for him who gives of his very soul and a compassion for the audience to whom we are writing, even though many of them may not fully agree with us.

Thirdly, *consistency*. O how I learned consistency! A double minded man gets nothing from the Lord, and a dou-ble minded man can have no influence through the printed page. Well, Dad, a closed mouth gathers no foot. I am still eating it, but how I praise God!

The Victorian Fade Out

*An unedited manuscript by James L. Johnson
written in the early seventies*

*S*o what's my bag? The bearded young Turk who carried my belongings to my hotel room wanted to know. "To find out how to communicate to Londoners," I told him. He looked like an exact double of the Smith Brothers on the cough drop box. And I detected a bit of Scottish in his tongue.

"Then visit the shrines," he said abruptly, not bothering to ask me why I wanted to communicate, so stealing my opportunity to tell him that it was to present God in a more meaningful way. He dropped my bags inside the door, and I handed him a ten shilling note. He looked at it, then at me, like I was Bertrand Russell himself, or even maybe one of the Beatles and added, "You might be keepin' your eyes open. And don't forget Soho."

I really had expected more from him. I didn't want to see the shrines again, and what had the notorious Soho to do with it? But the next day I took his advice for want of a better way to attack. I had been this route before—Trafalgar, Nelson's Column, Whitehall, the Tower, Westminster, the whole "Victorian London" bit.

I remembered the last time two years ago—it had been a wonderful history lesson; the people quiet and respectful like it was a cemetery, and over it a kind of loneliness and coldness, since historical shrines never gave off much heat. And always those constantly visible thumbprints of the past, as if the marble statues came to life at night and played their games while the city slept. "Take away the shrines, and London sinks into the sea," a bitter Cockney cab driver told me on the way in from the airport. "Like pulling a dozen or so corks out of the bottom of the boat, heh?"

I didn't know about that, and I doubted it was that easy.

I hit Trafalgar Square first, this time "keeping my eyes open." It was the same it seemed—the usual peanut shells all over the place, pigeons, fountains, and the inevitable statues frozen in their still photography. But there was something else today. There were girls in micro-minis and boys in ragged edged shorts dancing in circles. Their message was plain enough, but the sign made it plainer: "Let your sex be free!"

It wouldn't last long—the bobbies would be there soon to break it up. But the people who passed, the people who demanded respect and no noise, didn't turn their heads in embarrassment like they used to. Now they stood and watched, some with glum faces, some with reluctant smiles, not sure what to make of it. And the gay sounds seemed to crack ominously on the images of stone and turn the flat splashing water of the fountains into lilting giggles. I watched, wondered, and finally moved on.

At Nelson's Column off Whitehall, on top of which Lord Nelson perched like a watchman looking for whales, I mused with others what the glory of the British fleet once was. But at the base of the column was a crude sign done in a childlike scrawl which said, "Nelson is not God—John Lennon is!"

At Westminster Abbey, where a London Teddy boy told me a long time ago that "the dead never had it so good," a handful of teenagers, barefoot, in levis, leather jackets, and sun glasses carried signs that said: "Let the dead bury their dead—and come feed the poor!"

In the Tower of London, Henry VIII stood stiffly in his black stone armor, and in his left hand someone had put a red geranium, gone unnoticed apparently by the guards.

In Madam Tussard's Wax Museum that captured all the horrible criminals and crimes of the past in realistic, frozen pantomime, someone had slipped a paper sign on the chain around Jack the Ripper which said: "Love could have saved him!"

And everywhere I went there seemed to be some sly little mark of protest, someone trying to get attention for something else that was missing in these trophy rooms.

Finally, when the sun went down and the lights came on strong in Picadilly Circus, I sat under the Statue of Eros, pondering my next move to Soho. While I sat, a young girl in a faded trench coat sat down next to me. She shivered with the sharp night air and leaned toward me like she wanted protection. "I can't think of a better beginning, ducks, than under Eros, can you now?"

She was too young for that, not more than fourteen maybe, and new at it, too, for she almost fluffed the line. And her eyes carried the lie, too—mostly hoping I'd say no, afraid to face it, and hoping I'd say yes . . . because this was her way of life now, the gay life. I said, "How about talk instead?" She seemed confused by that, then got up and walked on.

Around eleven o'clock I toured Soho, a notorious square mile of Honky Tonk and Sodom and Gomorrah all thrown together. Everything and anything was for sale—from Italian sausage to burlesque to dope. Music and laughter went together, but it sounded tinny and unreal like it came out of the organ grinder.

Outside one purplish looking pub, a girl came up to me and said, "Which way will you go to the moon, love? Grass or sex?" She was maybe nineteen, but her face was deathly waxy in color. I said, "Neither, but how about some talk?"

"Too bourgeois, that," she countered with a huff. "We come here to live, not die."

It was near midnight when I walked alone on the quieter streets of old London. I knew now why that young Turk said to see the shrines. If I was going to communicate God here, I would have to reckon with the fact that old Victorian London was doing a slow fade. Statues and war memorials and wax works of horror had no love. Instead, something else was fading in over it—shivering girls plying the trade to find something meaningful, an army of sign boards and graffiti and wilted geraniums and boys and girls chasing Eros for the "good life."

And I turned to look back once before getting into the cab and saw the imposing dome of St. Paul's Cathedral standing out against the sky . . . it had taken all that the Luftwaffe could throw at it once . . . but now it, too, was a museum full of relics of another day of glory. Now—lifeless and cold.

And then Big Ben began tolling its midnight hour, and I waited, respectfully listening like I was at a grave side, until it finished. The day was done.

Living Philosophy

An unedited manuscript by James L. Johnson
Written in 1981

*I*t was George Eliot who said,

> "Tis God gives skill,
> But not without men's hands; He
> could not make
> Antonio Stradivari's violins
> Without Antonio."

Lest we conclude that God can do very well without us—and I am sure He can if He wishes to—I remember someone in history who said, "God has confined himself to a million deputies."

I had my first lesson in what we ought to be doing with our hands when I was nine years old. My elder brother, ten years my senior, and I were on our Michigan farm bagging potatoes . . . that night as we camped there, a vicious September thunderstorm ripped across and dumped torrential rains on us. When we arose the next morning and headed for home, we found the bridge had been washed out, and the little ditch had become a wide crevasse with water rushing through it.

My brother, being strong and ingenious, found a log and dropped it across the ditch. Boldly he walked the log to the other side and turned to wait for me. I, however, was too frightened to move, my eyes on that chasm and that churning water. Seeing my hesitancy, my brother walked back over the log half-way and knelt down and reached out his big, calloused, lumberjack hands to me and said, "Don't look down; just look at my hands, and keep yours in mine."

Still terrified, I moved out slowly, keeping my eyes fixed on those hands as he ordered. I simply put my small ones in his, and he finally led me across to safety.

That lesson should have served notice that life is to be lived in reaching out to others to help them across the many terrifying chasms of life.

Unfortunately for me, I did not take it to heart . . . for 25 years I did not give my hands to anyone to help; nor did I take anyone else's unless there was some *thing* in them I wanted. I kept reaching for things and not for somebody, taking instead of giving.

I started writing when I was 12 years old but wrote not so much in the ensuing years to give my hands to anyone in that writing but to hopefully win the Pulitzer Prize or write the great American novel.

In the Navy during World War II, where you lived on helping each other, I was forever looking out for myself . . . I kept my hand on the life boat or the life raft at all times . . . because I figured when the time came I'd at least be first.

But through all of this kind of living I knew there had to be something better, something more, something more fulfilling . . . but as much as I wanted to be someone other than a grabber, I could not rise to it. I had no power to change.

Finally in 1951 in Moody Church in Chicago, I came face-to-face with the bankruptcy of my life. That night I realized for the first time that I had spent my 25 years in selfish living.

Torn inside and empty and confused, I caught what Jesus said to the man with the withered hand recorded in Mark three. "Stretch forth thine hand," He told the man. "And the man stretched it out; and his hand was restored whole as the other."

That night my withered hands and heart were healed ... and from that night on I started using them for God; I went to Africa with my wife to lift people there spiritually. I served two pastorates at home with the same intent. I began writing after that, not for glory or gold, but for the satisfaction of helping someone else live again. I went into teaching, not to get something from my students so much but to give to them the help they needed to go on and find their niche in Christian service . . .

And then one night two years ago, when I lay dying after open heart surgery hundreds of people reached out their hands for me in prayer . . . and in the midst of that darkness God was there, putting out His hands to me and saying, "Don't look down, just keep your eyes on my hands and I will lead you over . . ."

And He did . . . my living philosophy is not complicated any more than the Christian life is complicated in this regard. I simply have, like Antonio Stradivari, given my hands to the perfecting of what God wants to perfect through me. It has been a 30-year journey rich with rewards and fulfillment, and I thank Him for it.

Jim's Last Word

Written by Jim Johnson in May 1987
in preparation for his funeral service

I've always tried to get it as you all know. Maybe I will have it now, since you have no choice.

"Do not go gently into this good-night." I don't know who said it, but I guess I fulfilled it in a way to the end. I have never done anything in life very "gently" anyway, even slowing up for a red light. No point doing it on the last leg. Still, I hope I haven't embarrassed anyone in the way I went . . . I hope I gave death a bit of a bloody nose. But then maybe I whimpered all the way home, God forbid . . . if so, I hope you don't think too harshly of me . . . for we all cross this way but once and none of us can know what emotion shall dominate our final hours . . .

It was a good life. Good with Rosemary and Jay and you all . . . not enough time with them, though, not enough quality time. For that I am truly sorry. For all I went through in that heart surgery, I thought I learned what or why quality time with those closest to you was all about. I didn't. But now it is too late to review . . . it is always too late when we wait.

Accomplishments don't mean much now . . . God will review that later. But I feel singly blessed in writing and publishing those 14 books, for the years of teaching, for the many rich hours ministering as a missionary, and a director of literature development overseas. I had good friends . . . helpful, encouraging, forbearing. Thank you for being all of those to me.

I simply leave to you whatever good memories there might be of those times we all had time to reach out and touch and listen and laugh . . . far too brief. Thank you for that too.

I am grateful I came to know Christ at the age of 25 and was privileged to live for Him—though I do not cherish those times when I did not do that very well—and to serve Him. He confronted me in February 18, 1951 at Moody Church in Chicago after many other encounters which did not "take." Type A's don't stick around long to catch the significance of the mysteries of the universe . . . but on that night all of the exposure to the Scriptures back in those Lutheran Church days of my youth came to full vision . . . all of the testimonies of others to the reality of Christ came to fruition. I was finally "in."

Without that experience, I could not write this with any sense of expectation of what is yet to come with Him, nor could I have every produced a solitary word, speech, sermon, or act of love to someone else in the genuine sense of that word. Man is simply incapable of rising to that dimension in himself.

Well . . . let's not get too windy here.

For those of you who have taken the time to make this last farewell, thank you. For those who have come to dwell on what I was that didn't necessarily come up to your expectations, thank you too. For we all measure the departure of another each in our own way . . . and there is no perfect person in terms of meeting our criteria for "perfect," right?

Thanks to you few precious souls for bearing with me, for not chiding me too harshly on my failures . . . and being so very kind to prod me on to whatever I was supposed to accomplish in this all too short sojourn.

Take time to smell the roses . . . I failed to do that as much as I should. Don't forget to walk a mile every day. I didn't, so now you know how important that is. Take time to look at the stars on those warm July nights . . . and those beautiful winter nights when all of the galaxies are like crystal . . . the kiss of setting sun on green grass or white snow . . . the flush of greenery in spring, the majestic finalities of fall . . .

And let God have His rightful place at your side in that. To amplify the images, the sounds, whisper of the good earth quietly breathing around you . . . then you will be closer than ever to the reality of His Being.

Do not judge those of your brethren or sisters who fail . . . certainly they deserve some acknowledgment of their human frailty. Heal the broken hearted, pick up the downtrodden, love them all as Christ loved you, all of us.

Good-bye for now . . . see you at the Eastern Gate! And we'll compare notes.

Finally, *Ex Umbris et Imaginibus in Veritatem!* From shadows and symbols into the truth. Now I shall know!

To my wife, Rosemary, I leave this tribute that says it better than I:

> I fill this cup to one made up
> Of loveliness alone,
> A woman, of her gentle sex
> The seeming paragon;
> To whom the better elements
> And kindly stars have given
> A form so fair, that, like the air,
> 'Tis less of earth than heaven.

> —Edward Coate Pinkney

To my son, Jay:

> Not of the sunlight,
> Not of the moonlight,
> Not of the starlight!
> O young Mariner,
> Down to the haven,
> Call your companions,
> Launch your vessel,
> And crowd your canvas,
> And, ere it vanishes
> Over the margin,
> After it, follow it,
> Follow the Gleam.

> —Alfred Lord Tennyson

Moody Press, a ministry of the Moody Bible Institute,
is designed for education, evangelization, and edification.
If we may assist you in knowing more about Christ
and the Christian life, please write us without obligation:
Moody Press, c/o MLM, Chicago, Illinois 60610.